THE ACTRESS

Dans la même collection :

Ray Bradbury
A Story of Love
The Last Circus and Interviews
The Martian Chronicles

Agatha Christie
A Fruitful Sunday and other Short Stories

Roald Dahl
Someone Like You and Other Short Stories
The Hitch-Hiker and Other Short Stories

Graham Greene
The Third Man

Mary Higgins Clark
Terror Stalks the Class Reunion

James Joyce
Dubliners

Ruth Rendell
Walter's Leg and Other Short Stories

Collectifs
English Crime Stories of Today
English Ghost Stories
Nine English Short Stories
Thirteen Modern English and American Short Stories
The Umbrella Man and Other Short Stories (premières lectures)

Collection « Lire en anglais »
fondée par Henri Yvinec

Agatha Christie

The Actress
and Other Short Stories

Annotations par Chantal Yvinec
Professeur certifié d'anglais

Le Livre de Poche

© Librairie Générale Française, 2006,
pour les notes et présentations.

ISBN : 978-2-253-08404-4 – 1re publication

Sommaire

Abbreviations

adj	adjective
adv	adverb
cf	confer (see)
excl	exclamation
fam	familiar
fem	feminine
fml	formal
masc	masculine
pl	plural *(pluriel)*
qqch	*quelque chose*
qq'un	*quelqu'un*
sing	singular *(singulier)*
s.o	someone
sthg	something

=	synonym
≠	antonym or different meaning from (underlined word) means "watch out!"

La collection « Lire en anglais »

Tout naturellement, après quelques années d'étude d'une langue étrangère, naît l'envie de découvrir sa littérature. Mais le vocabulaire dont on dispose est souvent insuffisant ; la perspective de recherches lexicales multipliées chez le lecteur isolé, la présentation fastidieuse du vocabulaire, pour le professeur, sont autant d'obstacles redoutables. C'est pour tenter de les aplanir que nous proposons cette collection. Elle constitue une étape vers la lecture autonome, sans dictionnaire ni traduction, grâce à des notes facilement repérables.

Le lecteur trouvera :

En page de gauche
Des textes de grands auteurs contemporains, pour la plupart, choisis pour leur intérêt littéraire et la qualité de leur langue.

En page de droite
Des notes juxtalinéaires rédigées dans la langue du texte, qui aident le lecteur à :

Comprendre
Tous les mots et expressions difficiles contenus dans la ligne de gauche sont reproduits en caractères gras et expliqués dans le contexte ;

Observer
Des notes d'observation de la langue soulignent la caractère idiomatique de certaines tournures ou constructions ;

Apprendre

Dans un but d'enrichissement lexical, certaines notes proposent enfin des synonymes, des antonymes, des expressions faisant appel aux mots qui figurent dans le texte.

C'est à dessein que quelques mots clés sont expliqués plus d'une fois. Ils sont alors présentés sous un autre angle, notamment à l'aide de nouveaux synonymes ou antonymes, plus adéquats dans un nouvel épisode de l'histoire. Ceci pourra également éviter des retours en arrière toujours fastidieux.

Vocabulaire en contexte

En fin de volume, une liste importante de mots contenus dans le texte, suivis de leur traduction, comporte, entre autres, les verbes irréguliers et les mots qui n'ont pas été annotés faute de place ou parce que leur sens était évident dans le contexte. Grâce à ce lexique, on pourra, en dernier recours, procéder à quelques vérifications ou faire un bilan des mots retenus au cours des lectures.

Henri Yvinec

About Agatha Christie
(Torquay, 1891 – Wallingford, 1976)

Agatha Christie's reputation as a writer of detective stories has crossed generations and borders. Indeed, her books have been translated into all major foreign languages and she is the third most widely published author of all times, after the Bible and Shakespeare.

Although some writers have claimed or have been awarded the title since her time, Agatha Christie remains the original Queen of Crime. She invented a new approach to the detective novel, concentrating on the characters' motives rather than on the crime itself. Her name evokes brilliant intricate plots, clever suspense and, of course, the surprise ending which even the most imaginative reader cannot foresee!

Even if they deal with criminal affairs, her stories are never bloody. Their interest lies mainly in the psychological study of the characters and they have a refined touch and the charm of old England where they are set.

Two of Agatha Christie's heroes have reached world fame: Hercule Poirot, the meticulous little Belgian detective with the egg-shaped head and the moustache and Miss Marple – Agatha Christie's own favourite heroine – the exquisite 'so British' old lady who has a great talent in understanding human nature.

During her career, which lasted over half a century, Agatha Christie wrote 67 novels, around 150 short stories, 19 plays, two books of poetry, another book of poems and children's stories, as well as an autobiography and an account of the expeditions she shared with her second husband, the archaeologist Sir Max Mallowan. She also wrote six books under the pseudonym of Mary Westmacott. Two of her novels have been published posthumously, at her request: *Curtain*, in which Hercule Poirot is killed and *Sleeping Murder*, Miss Marple's last case.

N. B: Les mots difficiles de cette introduction figurent dans le lexique en fin de volume.

The Actress

The shabby man in the fourth row of the pit leant forward and stared incredulously at the stage. His shifty eyes narrowed furtively.

'Nancy Taylor!' he muttered. 'By the Lord, little Nancy Taylor!'

His glance dropped to the programme in his hand. One name was printed in slightly larger type than the rest.

'Olga Stormer! So that's what she calls herself. Fancy yourself a star, don't you, my lady? And you must be making a pretty little pot of money, too. Quite forgotten your name was ever Nancy Taylor, I dare say. I wonder now – I wonder now what you'd say if Jake Levitt should remind you of the fact?'

The curtain fell on the close of the first act. Hearty applause filled the auditorium. Olga Stormer, the great emotional actress, whose name in a few short years had become a household word, was adding yet another triumph to her list of successes as 'Cora', in *The Avenging Angel*.

Jake Levitt did not join in the clapping, but a slow, appreciative grin gradually distended his mouth. God! What luck! Just when he was on his beam-ends, too. She'd try to bluff it out, he supposed, but she couldn't put it over on *him*. Properly worked, the thing was a gold-mine!

On the following morning the first workings of Jake Levitt's gold-mine became apparent. In her drawing-room, with its red lacquer and black hangings, Olga Stormer read and re-read a letter thoughtfully. Her pale face, with its exquisitely mobile features, was a little more set than usual, and every now and then the grey-green eyes under the level brows steadily envisaged the middle distance, as though she contemplated the threat behind rather than the actual words of the letter.

In that wonderful voice of hers which could throb with

shabby: inelegant ● **fourth row:** 4th line of seats ● orchestra
pit ● **leant:** bent ● **stared:** looked fixedly ● actors act on a **stage**
shifty: moving fast ● **narrowed:** became smaller
muttered: said to himself ● **By the Lord!:** excl. of surprise

his glance dropped to: he looked at; glance: brief look
printed: written ● **slightly:** a little ● **larger type:** bigger letters
what she calls herself: her name as an artist, her stage name
● **fancy:** imagine
a pretty little pot (fam): a big sum ● **quite forgotten:** you don't
remember ● **I dare say:** I suppose ● **I wonder:** I ask myself
you'd: you would (conditional) ● **if** (condition) ● **remind you**
(evokes a flashback): make your remember
the curtain falls **on the close** (= the end) of an act at the theatre
hearty applause: vigourous clapping of the hands ● **filled:**
invaded ● **in a few short years:** very rapidly (one **year** = 365
days) ● **a household word:** famous; well-known ● **adding** (to a
list) ● **as:** in the role of ● **avenging:** taking her revenge
clapping: applause
grin: smile of satisfaction ● **God!:** excl. of surprise ● **luck:** good
fortune ● **on his beam-ends** (fam): short of money, with
no money left ● **put it over on him:** bluff him; cheat on him
properly worked: with a well-organised plan ● **a gold-mine:** a
fabulous source of money
following: next ● **workings:** results
drawing-room: sitting-room; lounge
hangings: draperies hanging on each side of the window;
curtains ● **thoughtfully:** pensively
features: parts of the face ● **set:** immobile ● **every now and
then:** occasionally ● **level:** regular ● **brows:** lines of hair
above the eyes ● **steadily:** fixedly ● **envisaged:** looked at
contemplated: imagined ● **threat:** menace ● **actual:** real
wonderful: marvellous ● **throb:** vibrate

emotion or be as clear-cut as the click of a type-writer, Olga called: 'Miss Jones!'

A neat young woman with spectacles, a shorthand pad and a pencil clasped in her hand, hastened from an adjoining room.

'Ring up Mr Danahan, please, and ask him to come round, immediately.'

Syd Danahan, Olga Stormer's manager, entered the room with the usual apprehension of the man whose life it is to deal with and overcome the vagaries of the artistic feminine. To coax, to soothe, to bully, one at a time or all together, such was his daily routine. To his relief, Olga appeared calm and composed, and merely flicked a note across the table to him.

'Read that.'

The letter was scrawled in an illiterate hand, on cheap paper.

> *'Dear Madam,*
> *I much appreciated your performance in* The Avenging Angel *last night. I fancy we have a mutual friend in Miss Nancy Taylor, late of Chicago. An article regarding her is to be published shortly. If you would care to discuss same, I could call upon you at any time convenient to yourself.*
> *Yours respectfully,*
>
> *Jake Levitt'*

Danahan looked slightly bewildered.

'I don't quite get it. Who is this Nancy Taylor?'

'A girl who would be better dead, Danny.' There was bitterness in her voice and a weariness that revealed her 34 years. 'A girl who was dead until this carrion crow brought her to life again.'

'Oh! Then…'

'Me, Danny. Just me.'

'This means blackmail, of course?'

clear-cut: distinct ● **type-writer:** machine used to type letters on

spectacles: old word for glasses ● **shorthand:** *sténographie*
pad: notebook ● **pencil** (to write with) ● **clasped:** held firmly
hastened: rushed, hurried
ring up: call on the telephone ● **come round:** come here

whose life it is: whose occupation consists in (cf daily routine,
below) ● **deal with and overcome:** take action on and solve
(problems) ● **vagaries:** caprices ● **coax, soothe, bully:**
encourage, comfort and put pressure on ● **daily:** everyday
● **relief:** deliverance after a moment of apprehension
● **composed:** self-controlled ● **merely:** simply ● **flicked:** passed
energetically
scrawled: badly written (difficult to read) ● **cheap:** of bad quality

performance: public show (of actors)
I fancy: I believe
late of Chicago: who lived in Chicago before
is to be: will be (future) ● **shortly:** soon ● **care to:** want, wish,
desire to ● **same:** thing already mentioned ● **call upon you:**
come and see you, pay you a visit
Yours respectfully: yours sincerely; yours faithfully (end of a letter)

bewildered: stupefied
I don't quite get it: I don't understand very well
who would be better dead: who should not exist any more
bitterness: strong resentment ● **weariness:** tiredness, fatigue
carrion crow: predatory bird that feeds on dead animals
or human bodies ● **brought her to life again:** revived her,
resurrected her

blackmail s.o: send letters of menace to s.o in order to obtain
money

She nodded. 'Of course, and by a man who knows the art thoroughly.'

Danahan frowned, considering the matter. Olga, her cheek pillowed on a long, slender hand, watched him with unfathomable eyes.

'What about bluff? Deny everything. He can't be sure that he hasn't been misled by a chance resemblance.'

Olga shook her head.

'Levitt makes his living by blackmailing women. He's sure enough.'

'The police?' hinted Danahan doubtfully.

Her faint, derisive smile was answer enough. Beneath her self-control, though he did not guess it, was the impatience of the keen brain watching a slower brain laboriously cover the ground it had already traversed in a flash.

'You don't – er – think it might be wise for you to – er – say something yourself to Sir Richard? That would partly spike his guns.'

The actress's engagement to Sir Richard Everard, MP, had been announced a few weeks previously.

'I told Richard everything when he asked me to marry him.'

'My word, that was clever of you!' said Danahan admiringly.

Olga smiled a little.

'It wasn't cleverness, Danny dear. You wouldn't understand. All the same, if this man Levitt does what he threatens, my number is up, and incidentally Richard's Parliamentary career goes smash, too. No, as far as I can see, there are only two things to do.'

'Well?'

'To pay – and that of course is endless! Or to disappear, start again.'

The weariness was again very apparent in her voice.

'It isn't even as though I'd done anything I regretted. I was a half-starved little gutter waif, Danny, striving to keep straight. I shot a man, a beast of a man who deserved to be shot. The circumstances under which I killed him were such

nodded: agreed with a sign of the head ● **the art** of blackmailing
thoroughly: perfectly well
frowned: showed perplexity on his face ● **matter:** question,
problem ● **her cheek** (= side of the face) **pillowed ...:** in the
attitude of s.o who is thinking ● **unfathomable:** mysterious
deny: declare it is false
misled: guided in a wrong direction ● **chance:** accidental
shake, **shook,** shaken **her head** to express her disapproval
makes his living: earns enough money to live

hinted: suggested ● **doubtfully:** with a lot of doubts, uncertain
faint: imperceptible ● **derisive:** cf derision ● **answer enough:**
eloquent ● **guess:** vaguely perceive, suppose
keen: quick, active ● **brain:** centre of intelligence ● **slower:** not
so fast ● **cover the ground:** examine the situation ● **in a flash:**
very fast ● **wise:** prudent

spike his guns: ruin his plans
engagement to get married ● **MP:** Member of Parliament
a few: not many ● **previously:** before
tell, **told,** told (a story): narrate, relate ● **marry him:** not <u>with</u> him!

My word!: excl. of admiration ● **clever:** intelligent

cleverness: intelligence ● **wouldn't:** can't, are unable to
threatens: menaces
my number is up: I am lost; my career is destroyed
goes smash: is ruined, is hopeless ● **as far as I can see:** in my
opinion

endless: having no end, never finishing

It isn't ... I regretted: I have no regrets at all
half-starved: hungry ● **waif:** abandoned child ● **striving:**
making efforts ● **keep straight:** not be a delinquent ● **shot** with
a gun ● **deserved:** merited ● **killed:** murdered

that no jury on earth would have convicted me. I know that now, but at the time I was only a frightened kid – and – I ran.'

Danahan nodded.

'I suppose,' he said doubtfully, 'there's nothing against this man Levitt we could get hold of?'

Olga shook her head.

'Very unlikely. He's too much of a coward to go in for evil-doing.' The sound of her own words seemed to strike her. 'A coward! I wonder if we couldn't work on that in some way.'

'If Sir Richard were to see him and frighten him,' suggested Danahan.

'Richard is too fine an instrument. You can't handle that sort of man with gloves on.'

'Well, let me see him.'

'Forgive me, Danny, but I don't think you're subtle enough. Something between gloves and bare fists is needed. Let us say mittens! That means a woman! Yes, I rather fancy a woman might do the trick. A woman with a certain amount of *finesse*, but who knows the baser side of life from bitter experience. Olga Stormer, for instance! Don't talk to me, I've got a plan coming.'

She leant forward, burying her face in her hands. She lifted it suddenly.

'What's the name of that girl who wants to understudy me? Margaret Ryan, isn't it? The girl with the hair like mine?'

'Her hair's all right,' admitted Danahan grudgingly, his eyes resting on the bronze-gold coil surrounding Olga's head. 'It's just like yours, as you say. But she's no good any other way. I was going to sack her next week.'

'If all goes well, you'll probably have to let her understudy "Cora".' She smothered his protests with a wave of her hand. 'Danny, answer me one question honestly. Do you think I can act? Really *act*, I mean. Or am I just an attractive woman who trails round in pretty dresses?'

'Act? My God! Olga, there's been nobody like you since Duse!'

on earth (intensifier) ● **convicted:** condemned
frightened: extremely anxious ● **kid** (fam): young child
run, **ran,** run: escaped

get hold of: find
shake, **shook,** shaken: moved (her head) from left to right
(meaning "no") ● **unlikely**: improbable ● **coward:** not courageous
evil-doing: performing actions that are not morally acceptable
strike, struck, struck: impress ● **work on that:** take advantage
of that
if (condition) ... **were** instead of "was"(conditional)

fine: subtle ● **handle:** deal with; treat
gloves: protection for the hands
let me: permit me to, allow me to
forgive me: pardon me
bare fists (with no gloves on!) ● **needed:** necessary
mittens: *mitaines* ● **that means:** the solution is (mean, meant,
meant) ● **do the trick:** be perfect for the situation ● **amount:**
degree ● **the baser side** ≠ the rosy aspect (of existence)
● **bitter:** difficult, harsh ● **for instance:** for example

burying: hiding; holding
lifted: raised (upward movement)
understudy: study a role and play as a substitute for an actor
mine (possessive pronoun to avoid repetition): like my hair
grudgingly ≠ voluntarily
bronze-gold: sort of blond colour ● **coil:** curl
any other way: in any other aspect
sack (fam)**:** dismiss ● **next week:** the coming week

smothered: rejected ● **wave:** movement (like a wave on the
sea) ● **I can:** I have the capacity or talent to
attractive: good-looking, pretty
trails round (doing nothing) ● **pretty:** nice, lovely
● **dress(es):** woman's article of clothing (long dress, evening
dress...)

'Then if Levitt is really a coward, as I suspect, the thing will come off. No, I'm not going to tell you about it. I want you to get hold of the Ryan girl. Tell her I'm interested in her and want her to dine here tomorrow night. She'll come fast enough.'

'I should say she would!'

'The other thing I want is some good strong knock-out drops, something that will put anyone out of action for an hour or two, but leave them none the worse the next day.'

Danahan grinned.

'I can't guarantee our friend won't have a headache, but there will be no permanent damage done.'

'Good! Run away now, Danny, and leave the rest to me.' She raised her voice: 'Miss Jones!'

The spectacled young woman appeared with her usual alacrity.

'Take down this, please.'

Walking slowly up and down, Olga dictated the day's correspondence. But one answer she wrote with her own hand.

Jake Levitt, in his dingy room, grinned as he tore open the expected envelope.

'Dear Sir,
I cannot recall the lady of whom you speak, but I meet so many people that my memory is necessarily uncertain. I am always pleased to help any fellow actress, and shall be at home if you will call this evening at nine o'clock.
Yours faithfully,

Olga Stormer'

Levitt nodded appreciatively. Clever note! She admitted nothing. Nevertheless she was willing to treat. The gold-mine was developing.

At nine o'clock precisely Levitt stood outside the door of the actress's flat and pressed the bell. No one answered the summons, and he was about to press it again when he realized that the door was not latched. He pushed the door

the thing will come off: our plan will be successful

interested in (note the preposition!)
dine: have dinner
fast enough: quickly
I should say she would!: I am sure she will!, I bet she will!
strong: having a considerable effect ● **knockout:** K.O
drops: small quantities of liquid usually used as medicine
none the worse: all right, unharmed, healthy
grinned: gave a large smile
headache: a pain in the head (also: toothache, stomachache...)

raised her voice: spoke louder (in order to call s.o)
spectacled (physical characteristic): who wears spectacles
(= glasses) ● **alacrity:** zeal
take down: write down in your notebook
up and down: from left to right and back again across the room
with her own hand: herself
dingy: dirty and poor ● tear, **tore,** torn **open:** opened without
care ● **expected:** awaited

Sir, Madam, Miss: polite ways of addressing a man, a woman, a
lady ● **recall:** remember; bring back to my mind ● **whom:** object
form of "who"
fellow actress: an actress like myself ● **shall:** another form for "will"
will: want to, wish to
Yours faithfully (cf p.15, Yours respectfully)

appreciatively: with admiration
nevertheless (expresses contradiction) ● **willing** ≠ hostile

stand, **stood,** stood: was present
flat (GB): apartment (US) ● **bell:** door bell; telephone bell, etc.
summons: call ● **about to:** ready to (expresses imminence)
latched: locked (with a key)

open and entered the hall. To his right was an open door leading into a brilliantly lighted room, a room decorated in scarlet and black. Levitt walked in. On the table under the lamp lay a sheet of paper on which were written the words:

'Please wait until I return. – O. Stormer.'

Levitt sat down and waited. In spite of himself a feeling of uneasiness was stealing over him. The flat was so very quiet. There was something eerie about the silence.

Nothing wrong, of course, how could there be? But the room was so deadly quiet; and yet, quiet as it was, he had the preposterous, uncomfortable notion that he wasn't alone in it. Absurd! He wiped the perspiration from his brow. And still the impression grew stronger. He wasn't alone! With a muttered oath he sprang up and began to pace up and down. In a minute the woman would return and then –

He stopped dead with a muffled cry. From beneath the black velvet hangings that draped the window a hand protruded! He stooped and touched it. Cold – horribly cold – a dead hand.

With a cry he flung back the curtains. A woman was lying there, one arm flung wide, the other doubled under her as she lay face downwards, her golden-bronze hair lying in dishevelled masses on her neck.

Olga Stormer! Tremblingly his fingers sought the icy coldness of that wrist and felt for the pulse. As he thought, there was none. She was dead. She had escaped him, then, by taking the simplest way out.

Suddenly his eyes were arrested by two ends of red cord finishing in fantastic tassels, and half hidden by the masses of her hair. He touched them gingerly; the head sagged as he did so, and he caught a glimpse of a horrible purple face. He sprang back with a cry, his head whirling. There was something here he did not understand. His brief glimpse of the face, disfigured as it was, had shown him one thing. This was murder, not suicide. The woman had been strangled and – she was not Olga Stormer!

right ≠ left ● **leading into:** opening onto
lighted (with lamps) ● **scarlet:** vivid red colour
lie, **lay,** lain: was placed
sheet: piece

wait (a minute); wait <u>for</u> me

in spite of himself: <u>in</u>vonluntarily ● **feeling:** sensation
uneasiness: anxiousness ● **stealing over:** seizing ● **quiet:**
silent ● **eerie:** mysteriously frightening
wrong ≠ (all)right
deadly (intensifier): extremely ● **yet** (term of contradiction)
preposterous: absurd, ridiculous ● **alone:** the only person
wiped: removed; dried ● **perspiration:** sweat ● **brow:** forehead
grow, **grew,** grown **stronger:** increased; became more and more
important ● **oath:** rude word, swear word ● **sprang up:** jumped
to his feet ● **pace:** walk
dead (intensifier): suddenly ● **muffled:** not audible ● **cry** of
horror, of fear ● **velvet:** *velours*
protruded: was coming out ● **stooped:** bent down
dead ≠ alive, living
fling, **flung,** flung **back:** drew back violently ● **lying** on the floor
flung wide: largely outstretched ● **doubled:** turned back
lie, **lay,** lain (cf lying, above) ● **downwards:** facing the ground
dishevelled: disorderly ● **neck:** joint between head and body
fingers (on the hands) ● seek, **sought**, sought (trying to feel)
● **icy:** cold as ice ● the **wrist** (between hand and arm) is where
the pulse (the blood pressure) can be **felt** (feel, felt, felt) ● **none**
(pronoun): no pulse ● **way out:** exit, departure
ends: extremities
tassels (for decoration): *glands* ● hide, hid, **hidden:** not visible
gingerly: carefully, delicately ● **sagged:** dropped
catch, **caught,** caught **a glimpse of:** had a quick look at
whirling: spinning (sensation of vertigo)
glimpse: vision

murder: homicide ● **strangled:** killed by strangulation of the
neck

Ah! What was that? A sound behind him. He wheeled round and looked straight into the terrified eyes of a maid-servant crouching against the wall. Her face was as white as the cap and apron she wore, but he did not understand the fascinated horror in her eyes until her half-breathed words enlightened him to the peril in which he stood.

'Oh, my God! You've killed 'er!'

Even then he did not quite realize. He replied:

'No, no, she was dead when I found her.'

'I saw yer do it! You pulled the cord and strangled her. I 'eard the gurgling cry she give.'

The sweat broke out upon his brow in earnest. His mind went rapidly over his actions of the previous few minutes. She must have come in just as he had the two ends of cord in his hands; she had seen the sagging head and had taken his own cry as coming from the victim. He stared at her helplessly. There was no doubting what he saw in her face – terror and stupidity. She would tell the police she had seen the crime committed, and no cross-examination would shake her, he was sure of that. She would swear away his life with the unshakable conviction that she was speaking the truth.

What a horrible, unforeseen chain of circumstances! Stop, was it unforeseen? Was there some devilry here? On an impulse he said, eyeing her narrowly:

'That's not your mistress, you know.'

Her answer, given mechanically, threw a light upon the situation.

'No, it's 'er actress friend – if you can call 'em friends, seeing that they fought like cat and dog. They were at it tonight, 'ammer and tongs.'

A trap! He saw it now.

'Where's your mistress?'

'Went out ten minutes ago.'

A trap! And he had walked into it like a lamb. A clever devil, this Olga Stormer; she had rid herself of a rival, and he was to suffer for the deed. Murder! My God, they hanged a man for murder! And he was innocent – innocent!

A stealthy rustle recalled him. The little maid was sidling

wheeled round: turned round (in order to look behind him)
straight: directly ● **maidservant:** female servant
crouching (in a state of prostration)
cap (on the head) **and apron** (over the clothes) ● wear, **wore,**
worn ● **half-breathed:** not clearly articulated
enlightened him to: made him realize
my God!: excl. of horror ● **'er:** for "her"
replied: answered
find, **found,** found
yer: fam. for "you"
'eard: for "heard" ● **gurgling:** noise made by s.o who is being
strangled ● **sweat:** perspiration ● **broke out:** appeared ● **in
earnest:** really ● **went over:** recapitulated ● **the previous
minutes:** the minutes before

stared at her: looked at her fixedly
helplessly: desperately

cross-examination: 2nd questioning ● **shake her:** make her
change her testimony ● **swear** (on her honour) **away his life:**
testify against him ● **unshakable:** firm ● **speaking the truth:**
telling what had <u>really</u> happened
unforeseen: unexpected, unpredicted ● **devilry:** action bearing
the mark of the devil (also called Satan) ● **eyeing:** observing
● **narrowly:** very closely, very well
throw, **threw,** thrown **a light upon:** helped him to understand

'em for "them"
seeing that: considering that ● fight, **fought,** fought: quarrelled
'ammer (for "hammer") **and tongs:** with great energy and noise
trap to catch s.o or sthg (mousetrap) ● see, **saw,** seen:
understood

lamb: young sheep; (figurative) innocent or naïve person
devil (cf devilry, above) ● **rid herself of:** become free by eliminating
deed: action (good deed; bad deed) ● **hanged:** killed by
suspending to rope tied around the neck; (hang, hung, hung or
hanged, hanged) ● **stealthy rustle:** very light sound ● **sidling:**

towards the door. Her wits were beginning to work again. Her eyes wavered to the telephone, then back to the door. At all costs he must silence her. It was the only way. As well hang for a real crime as a fictitious one. She had no weapon, neither had he. But he had his hands! Then his heart gave a leap. On the table beside her, almost under her hand, lay a small, jewelled revolver. If he could reach it first –

Instinct or his eyes warned her. She caught it up as he sprang and held it pointed at his breast. Awkwardly as she held it, her finger was on the trigger, and she could hardly miss him at that distance. He stopped dead. A revolver belonging to a woman like Olga Stormer would be pretty sure to be loaded.

But there was one thing, she was no longer directly between him and the door. So long as he did not attack her, she might not have the nerve to shoot. Anyway, he must risk it. Zig-zagging, he ran for the door, through the hall and out through the outer door, banging it behind him. He heard her voice, faint and shaky, calling, 'Police, Murder!' She'd have to call louder than that before anyone was likely to hear her. He'd got a start, anyway. Down the stairs he went, running down the open street, then slacking to a walk as a stray pedestrian turned the corner. He had his plan cut and dried. To Gravesend as quickly as possible. A boat was sailing from there that night for the remoter parts of the world. He knew the captain, a man who, for a consideration, would ask no questions. Once on board and out to sea he would be safe.

At eleven o'clock Danahan's telephone rang. Olga's voice spoke.

'Prepare a contract for Miss Ryan, will you? She's to understudy "Cora". It's absolutely no use arguing. I owe her something after all the things I did to her tonight! What? Yes, I think I'm out of my troubles. By the way, if she tells you tomorrow that I'm an ardent spiritualist and put her into a trance tonight, don't show open incredulity. How? Knock-out drops in the coffee, followed by scientific passes! After that I painted her face with purple grease paint and put a tourniquet

trying to escape secretly ● **wits:** brain, intelligence ● **work:**
function, operate ● **wavered:** moved hesitantly
at all costs (indicates that it is essential) ● **way:** solution ● **as
well hang:** it was better to be executed ● **weapon:** (fire) arm
neither had he: he had no weapon either ● **heart:** centre of
emotions ● **leap:** sudden jump ● **beside:** near, next to
jewelled: beautifully decorated ● **reach:** seize
warned her: informed her of his intention ● **caught it up:**
seized the revolver ● **sprang:** jumped ● **breast:** top front of the
body ● **awkwardly** ≠ dexterously ● you press the **trigger** of the
revolver to shoot (or fire) ● **... miss him:** she would certainly be
successful in shooting him ● **belonging to O. Stormer:** which
O. Stormer possessed ● **pretty sure** (expresses a certainty)
● **loaded** with ammunition
so long as: if; on condition that
nerve: courage
run, **ran,** run for: rushed to
banging: from "bang": noise heard when a door is shut violently
faint and shaky: feeble and hesitant
louder: with more intensity (loud voice ≠ low voice)
a start: a beginning
slacking: slowing down ● **stray:** rare ● **pedestrian:** person who
walks ● **cut and dried:** all ready
sailing on the sea, on a river... (sailing boat ≠ motor boat)
remoter parts of the world: places that are isolated from
civilisation ● **consideration:** sum of money given in exchange
for a service ● **safe:** out of danger

ring, **rang,** rung
speak, **spoke,** spoken: answered the call
will you? (polite phrase)
it's no use arguing: discussing is unnecessary ● **I owe her:** I'm
in debt to her
I'm out of my troubles: my problems have come to an end
a **spiritualist** (or medium) communicates with the spirits of the
dead ● **in a trance:** like a hypnotized person ● **open:** manifest

grease paint: special make-up for actors ● **tourniquet:** *garrot*

on her left arm! Mystified? Well, you must stay mystified until tomorrow. I haven't time to explain now. I must get out of the cap and apron before my faithful Maud returns from the pictures. There was a "beautiful drama" on tonight, she told me. But she missed the best drama of all. I played my best part tonight, Danny. The mittens won! Jake Levitt is a coward all right, and oh, Danny, Danny – I'm an actress!'

mystified: confused, puzzled, bewildered
get out of: remove, take off (clothes)
faithful: loyal
pictures: cinema ● **on:** being shown (on the screen)
missed: was absent for ● **the best** (superlative of "good")
part: role
a coward allright: really (a coward)

The Golden Ball

George Dundas stood in the City of London meditating.

All about him toilers and moneymakers surged and flowed like an enveloping tide. But George, beautifully dressed, his trousers exquisitely creased, took no heed of them. He was busy thinking what to do next.

Something had occurred! Between George and his rich uncle (Ephraim Leadbetter of the firm of Leadbetter and Gilling) there had been what is called in a lower walk of life 'words.' To be strictly accurate, the words had been almost entirely on Mr Leadbetter's side. They had flowed from his lips in a steady stream of bitter indignation, and the fact that they consisted almost entirely of repetition did not seem to have worried him. To say a thing once beautifully and then let it alone was not one of Mr Leadbetter's mottoes.

The theme was a simple one – the criminal folly and wickedness of a young man, who has his way to make, taking a day off in the middle of the week without even asking leave. Mr Leadbetter, when he had said everything he could think of and several things twice, paused for breath and asked George what he meant by it.

George replied simply that he had felt he wanted a day off. A holiday, in fact.

And what, Mr Leadbetter wanted to know, were Saturday afternoon and Sunday? To say nothing of Whitsuntide, not long past, and August Bank Holiday to come?

George said he didn't care for Saturday afternoons, Sundays or Bank Holidays. He meant a real day, when it might be possible to find some spot where half London was not assembled already.

Mr Leadbetter then said that he had done his best by his dead sister's son – nobody could say he hadn't given him a chance. But it was plain that it was no use. And in future

golden: made of (or the colour of) gold, a precious yellow metal

stand, **stood,** stood ● **the City:** London business centre
toilers; moneymakers: workers; business people ● **surged ...**
... tide: (image of a sea) there was a flow of people walking past
him ● **creased:** *repassé* ● take, **took,** taken **no heed of:** ignored
busy + ing: absorbed in ● **next:** after, later
occurred: happened, taken place
uncle (George is the nephew)
in a lower walk of life: among common (= ordinary) people
accurate: precise ● **almost:** nearly
... side: pronounced by Mr Leadbetter ● **flowed:** come out in a
flow ● **lips** (here: mouth) ● **steady stream:** regular flow ● **bitter:**
sarcastic
... worried him: had not been a problem for him ● **once:** one time
let it alone: stop there ● **mottoes:** rules of conduct
theme: subject
wickedness: very bad conduct ● **has his way to make:** must
build his career ● **a day off:** a day without working, a one-day
break ● **asking leave:** asking permission
twice: two times ● **for breath:** to breathe in air
meant by it: had in mind when he did it
felt: had the sensation
holiday: rest (= break) from work

to say nothing of: without mentioning ● **Whitsuntide:** Pentecost
Bank Holiday: official day when nobody works and banks are
closed ● **care for:** like, enjoy
mean, **meant,** meant
spot: place ● **half London:** half (50 %) the population of London

his best: the maximum he could do ● **by:** for the benefit of
dead ≠ alive, living ● **sister's son:** nephew ● give, gave, **given**
plain: clear ● **it was no use:** it didn't have any positive effect

George could have five real days with Saturday and Sunday added to do with as he liked.

'The golden ball of opportunity has been thrown up for you, my boy,' said Mr Leadbetter in a last touch of poetical fancy. 'And you have failed to grasp it.'

George said it seemed to him that that was just what he *had* done, and Mr Leadbetter dropped poetry for wrath and told him to get out.

Hence George – meditating. Would his uncle relent or would he not? Had he any secret affection for George, or merely a cold distaste?

It was just at that moment that a voice – a most unlikely voice – said, 'Hallo!'

A scarlet touring car with an immense long hood had drawn up to the curb beside him. At the wheel was that beautiful and popular society girl, Mary Montresor. (The description is that of the illustrated papers who produced a portrait of her at least four times a month.) She was smiling at George in an accomplished manner.

'I never knew a man could look so like an island,' said Mary Montresor. 'Would you like to get in?'

'I should love it above all things,' said George with no hesitation, and stepped in beside her.

They proceeded slowly because the traffic forbade anything else.

'I'm tired of the city,' said Mary Montresor. 'I came to see what it was like. I shall go back to London.'

Without presuming to correct her geography, George said it was a splendid idea. They proceeded sometimes slowly, sometimes with wild bursts of speed when Mary Montresor saw a chance of cutting in. It seemed to George that she was somewhat optimistic in the latter view, but he reflected that one could only die once. He thought it best, however, to essay no conversation. He preferred his fair driver to keep strictly to the job in hand.

It was she who reopened the conversation, choosing the moment when they were doing a wild sweep round Hyde Park Corner.

added: more, in addition ● **do with:** employ ● **liked:** wanted
The golden ball of opportunity (metaphor) **... for you:** you have had your chance
fancy: imagination ● **you have failed to grasp it:** you didn't catch it, you didn't take the opportunity
dropped poetry for wrath: changed from being lyrical to being really irritated ● **wrath:** anger ● **get out** (of the room): go away
Hence: so; as a result ● **would** (supposition) ● **relent:** become less cruel
merely: simply ● **distaste:** dislike
unlikely: improbable, unexpected
say, **said,** said
scarlet: bright red ● **hood:** front of a car ● **drawn up to:** stopped at ● **curb:** side of the road ● **beside:** near ● **at the wheel:** driving
society girl: woman belonging to the high society (= the upper class) ● **illustrated papers:** magazines ● **produced:** published
at least: at the minimum ● **smiling at:** addressing a smile (friendly expression on the face) to him ● **accomplished:** expert
knew: (here) imagined ● **like an island** (metaphor): alone, isolated ● **get in** ≠ get out
above all things: more than anything else
stepped in: got in
proceeded: drove ● **forbade:** did not permit

I'm tired of: I've had enough of
go back: return
presuming: taking the liberty of + ing

wild bursts of speed: sudden accelerations
chance: opportunity ● **cutting in:** forcing her way through the traffic ● **somewhat ... view** (euphemistic): she took some risks when doing that ● **die** (here) in a fatal accident ● **he thought it best**: he thought the best thing to do was ● **fair**: beautiful, pretty
the job in hand: (here) driving the car
she (subject) ● **choosing:** deciding on
wild sweep: sudden quick turn ● **Hyde Park** is the largest and most famous of London parks

'How would you like to marry me?' she inquired casually.

George gave a gasp, but that may have been due to a large bus that seemed to spell certain destruction. He prided himself on his quickness in response.

'I should love it,' he replied easily.

'Well,' said Mary Montresor vaguely. 'Perhaps you may someday.'

They turned into the straight without accident, and at that moment George perceived large new bills at Hyde Park Corner tube station. Sandwiched between GRAVE POLITICAL SITUATION and COLONEL IN DOCK, one said SOCIETY GIRL TO MARRY DUKE, and the other DUKE OF EDGEHILL AND MISS MONTRESOR.

'What's this about the Duke of Edgehill?' demanded George sternly.

'Me and Bingo? We're engaged.'

'But then – what you said just now –'

'Oh, *that*,' said Mary Montresor. 'You see, I haven't made up my mind who I shall actually marry.'

'Then why did you get engaged to him?'

'Just to see if I could. Everybody seemed to think it would be frightfully difficult, and it wasn't a bit!'

'Very rough luck on – er – Bingo,' said George, mastering his embarrassment at calling a real live duke by a nickname.

'Not at all,' said Mary Montresor. 'It will be good for Bingo, if anything *could* do him good – which I doubt.'

George made another discovery – again aided by a convenient poster.

'Why, of course, it's cup day at Ascot. I should have thought that was the one place you were simply bound to be today.'

Mary Montresor sighed.

'I wanted a holiday,' she said plaintively.

'Why, so did I,' said George, delighted. 'And as a result my uncle has kicked me out to starve.'

'Then in case we marry,' said Mary, 'my twenty thousand a year may come in useful?'

would you like to? (invitation) ● **marry me** (not <u>with</u> me!)
● **inquired:** asked ● **casually:** in a detached manner
gave a gasp: breathed with difficulty ● **may** (supposition) ● **due to:** caused by ● **spell certain destruction:** announce a fatal accident
● **prided:** was very proud of, satisfied with ● **quickness in response:** capacity to react rapidly ● **should** or would (conditional)
perhaps: possibly ● **may** (possibility)
someday or other
straight: road or street without any turning
bills: posters on the walls (for publicity)
tube: specific name for the London underground
in dock: in court (accused) ● **duke:** nobleman of high rank (fem. duchess)

sternly: severely
are engaged: have agreed to marry

make, **made,** made **up my mind:** decided
actually: really

frightfully: extremely, terribly ● **not a bit:** not at all
very rough luck on: what a pity for
mastering: not showing ● **real live:** still existing
nickname: familiar name used instead of the real name

do him good: benefit him
aided: helped ● **convenient:** opportune

why (excl.): well ● **cup:** trophy ● **Ascot:** place near London where a famous horse-race is held ● **one:** one and only ● **were bound to be:** would certainly be
sighed: let out a long deep breath

so did I: I did too ● **delighted:** very pleased ● **as a result:** consequently ● **kicked me out:** dismissed me ● **to starve:** with no means of subsistence ● **twenty thousand:** 20,000 (pounds sterling) ● **a year** or <u>per</u> year ● **come in useful:** be very welcome

'It will certainly provide us with a few home comforts,' said George.

'Talking of homes,' said Mary, 'let's go in the country and find a home we would like to live in.'

It seemed a simple and charming plan. They negotiated Putney Bridge, reached the Kingston by-pass and with a sigh of satisfaction Mary pressed her foot down on the accelerator. They got into the country very quickly. It was half an hour later that with a sudden exclamation Mary shot out a dramatic hand and pointed.

On the brow of a hill in front of them there nestled a house of what house agents describe (but seldom truthfully) as 'old-world charm.' Imagine the description of most houses in the country really come true for once, and you get an idea of this house.

Mary drew up outside a white gate.

'We'll leave the car and go up and look at it. It's our house!'

'Decidedly, it's our house,' agreed George. 'But just for the moment other people seem to be living in it.'

Mary dismissed the other people with a wave of her hand. They walked up the winding drive together. The house appeared even more desirable at close quarters.

'We'll go and peep in at all the windows,' said Mary.

George demurred.

'Do you think the other people –'

'I shan't consider them. It's our house – they're only living in it by a sort of accident. Besides, it's a lovely day and they're sure to be out. And if anyone does catch us, I shall say – I shall say – that I thought it was Mrs – Mrs Pardonstenger's house, and that I am so sorry I made a mistake.'

'Well, that ought to be safe enough,' said George reflectively.

They looked in through windows. The house was delightfully furnished. They had just got to the study when footsteps crunched on the gravel behind them and they turned to face a most irreproachable butler.

'Oh!' said Mary. And then putting on her most enchanting

provide us with + noun: supply us with, give us ● **a few home comforts:** a comfortable life in a well-equipped house ("a few" is euphemistic, here) ● **home:** house ● **let's** (invitation) ● **country** ≠ city
plan: project ● **negotiated:** drove across
a **bridge** goes over a river ● **reached:** arrived at ● **by-pass:** road taking the traffic round the city

later: after ● shoot, **shot,** shot **out a dramatic hand:** extended her hand in a theatrical gesture ● **pointed** (her hand) in order to indicate sthg ● **brow:** top ● **hill:** elevation of land ● **nestled:** was comfortably set ● **house agents** sell houses ● **seldom:** rarely ● **truthfully:** sincerely ● **old-world charm:** charm of ancient times
come true: become reality ● **for once:** just this time

drew up: stopped ● **gate:** barrier at the entrance
leave the car: get off the car and walk ● **go up** the alley (or drive)

dismissed: rejected ● **wave:** large gesture
winding: sinuous ● **drive:** alley ● **together** ≠ separately
at close quarters: when seen from very near
peep: look secretly
demurred: objected

shan't: shall not (future)
by accident: by chance ● **besides:** in addition
out: absent ● **does** catch (emphatic): catches, discovers
think**, thought,** thought
so + adj: very ● **mistake:** error
ought to: should (supposition) ● **safe** ≠ risky, dangerous

delightfully: beautifully ● **furnished** with tables, chairs, beds, etc.
study: room used for work ● **footsteps:** noise made by feet when walking ● **crunched:** made a crisp noise ● **gravel:** mixture of stones and sand ● **butler:** chief male servant of a house

smile, she said, 'Is Mrs Pardonstenger in? I was looking to see if she was in the study.'

'Mrs Pardonstenger is at home, madam,' said the butler. 'Will you come this way, please.'

They did the only thing they could. They followed him. George was calculating what the odds against this happening could possibly be. With a name like Pardonstenger he came to the conclusion it was about one in twenty thousand. His companion whispered, 'Leave it to me. It will be all right.'

George was only too pleased to leave it to her. The situation, he considered, called for feminine finesse.

They were shown into a drawing room. No sooner had the butler left the room than the door almost immediately reopened and a big florid lady with peroxide hair came in expectantly.

Mary Montresor made a movement towards her, then paused in well-simulated surprise.

'Why!' she exclaimed. 'It isn't Amy! What an extraordinary thing!'

'It *is* an extraordinary thing,' said a grim voice.

A man had entered behind Mrs Pardonstenger, an enormous man with a bulldog face and a sinister frown. George thought he had never seen such an unpleasant brute. The man closed the door and stood with his back against it.

'A very extraordinary thing,' he repeated sneeringly. 'But I fancy we understand your little game!' He suddenly produced what seemed an outsize in revolvers. 'Hands up. Hands up, I say. Frisk 'em, Bella.'

George in reading detective stories had often wondered what it meant to be frisked. Now he knew. Bella (alias Mrs P.) satisfied herself that neither he nor Mary concealed any lethal weapons on their persons.

'Thought you were mighty clever, didn't you?' sneered the man. 'Coming here like this and playing the innocents. You've made a mistake this time – a bad mistake. In fact, I very much doubt whether your friends and relations will ever see you again. Ah! You would, would you?' as George

in: here ≠ absent, away

madam: polite way of addressing a lady; "Sir" for a man
will you (polite request): would you like to ● **this way:** in this direction ● **followed:** went after
the odds against this happening: the probabilities for this to happen
one in twenty thousand: 1 chance out of 20,000
whispered: said in a low voice ● **leave it to me:** don't interfere

called for: asked for, required
they were shown into (note the passive form!) ● **drawing-room:** sitting-room ● **no sooner... than:** immediately after
florid: flamboyant ● **peroxide:** artificially blonde
expectantly: wanting to know what was happening
towards her: in her direction
well-simulated: fake

grim: severe, sinister

frown: hostile look on the face
unpleasant: disagreable, unfriendly
back ≠ front
sneeringly: with irony and disdain
game: stratagem
outsize: enormous ● **hands up** (order): put your hands up in the air ● **frisk' em** (for "them") (fam): search them to see if they hold no firearms ● **wondered:** asked himself
meant: represented
satisfied herself: made sure ● **neither ... nor:** *ni ... ni*
concealed: hid ● **lethal:** that can cause death ● **weapons:** firearms ● **thought** (elliptic): you thought ● **mighty** + adj (intensifier): very
bad: (here) serious, real
I doubt whether: I don't think
would do it (elliptic)

made a movement. 'None of your games. I'd shoot you as soon as look at you.'

'Be careful, George,' quavered Mary.

'I shall,' said George with feeling. 'Very careful.'

'And now march,' said the man. 'Open the door, Bella. Keep your hands above your heads, you two. The lady first – that's right. I'll come behind you both. Across the hall. Upstairs…'

They obeyed. What else could they do? Mary mounted the stairs, her hands held high. George followed. Behind them came the huge ruffian, revolver in hand.

Mary reached the top of the staircase and turned the corner. At the same moment, without the least warning, George lunged out a fierce backward kick. He caught the man full in the middle and he capsized backwards down the stairs. In a moment George had turned and leaped down after him, kneeling on his chest. With his right hand, he picked up the revolver which had fallen from the other's hand as he fell.

Bella gave a scream and retreated through a baize door. Mary came running down the stairs, her face as white as paper.

'George, you haven't killed him?'

The man was lying absolutely still. George bent over him.

'I don't think I've killed him,' he said regretfully. 'But he's certainly taken the count all right.'

'Thank God.' She was breathing rapidly.

'Pretty neat,' said George with permissible self-admiration. 'Many a lesson to be learnt from a jolly old mule. Eh, what?'

Mary pulled at his hand.

'Come away,' she cried feverishly. 'Come away quick.'

'If we had something to tie this fellow up with,' said George, intent on his own plans. 'I suppose you couldn't find a bit of rope or cord anywhere?'

'No, I couldn't,' said Mary. 'And come away, please – please – I'm so frightened.'

shoot, shot, shot: kill with a revolver

be careful: take care ● **quavered:** said with a trembling voice
feeling: emotion
march: walk with a military step

both: the two of you

mounted: went up
hold, **held**, held: raised ● **high** in the air
huge: massive, enormous ● **ruffian**: brute, villain
top ≠ bottom ● **staircase:** set of stairs (leading to bedrooms)
the least: the slightest ● **warning:** notification, announcement
lunged out a kick: violently struck (him) with his foot ● **caught:**
hit ● **capsized:** (here) fell; (of a boat) turn over
leaped: jumped
kneeling: pressing with his knee ● **chest:** upper front of the body
fall, fell, **fallen** on the floor
scream: loud cry; yell ● **baize door:** door padded with a thick
green material (for insulation) ● **as ... as** (comparison)

still: immobile ● bend, **bent,** bent: inclined his body

he's taken the count (boxing term): he has been knocked out
(= K.O) ● **Thank God:** excl. of relief
pretty neat (fam): quite well done
many <u>a</u> (emphatic) ● **a <u>jolly old</u>** (intensifiers) ● **mule:** young
female donkey (animal known for its vicious backward kick!)
pulled at his hand: took him by the hand to guide him somewhere
away: far from this place ● **cried:** shouted ● **feverishly:** excitedly
tie (up): attach ● **fellow** (fam): man
intent on: concentrating on
rope: thick cord

frightened: afraid

'You needn't be frightened,' said George with manly arrogance. '*I'm* here.'

'Darling George, please – for my sake. I don't want to be mixed up in this. Please let's go.'

The exquisite way in which she breathed the words 'for my sake' shook George's resolution. He allowed himself to be led forth from the house and hurried down the drive to the waiting car. Mary said faintly: 'You drive. I don't feel I can.' George took command of the wheel.

'But we've got to see this thing through,' he said. 'Heaven knows what blackguardism that nasty-looking fellow is up to. I won't bring the police into it if you don't want me to – but I'll have a try on my own. I ought to be able to get on their track all right.'

'No, George, I don't want you to.'

'We have a first-class adventure like this, and you want me to back out of it? Not on my life.'

'I'd no idea you were so bloodthirsty,' said Mary tearfully.

'I'm not bloodthirsty. I didn't begin it. The damned cheek of the fellow – threatening us with an outsize revolver. By the way – why on earth didn't that revolver go off when I kicked him downstairs?'

He stopped the car and fished the revolver out of the side pocket of the car where he had placed it. After examining it, he whistled.

'Well, I'm damned! The thing isn't loaded. If I'd known that –' He paused, wrapped in thought. 'Mary, this is a very curious business.'

'I know it is. That's why I'm begging you to leave it alone.'

'Never,' said George firmly.

Mary uttered a heart-rending sigh.

'I see,' she said, 'that I shall have to tell you. And the worst of it is that I haven't the least idea how you'll take it.'

'What do you mean – tell me?'

'You see, it's like this.' She paused. 'I feel girls should

needn't: (here) mustn't ● **manly:** typical of a man

darling (affectionate term) ● **for my sake:** for my benefit or satisfaction ● **mixed up:** involved
breathed: pronounced
shake, **shook,** shaken: changed ● **allowed:** let
be led forth (passive form): be guided out of ● **hurried:** ran, rushed ● **faintly:** in a low voice

see this thing through: finish what we have started ● **Heaven knows:** God knows ● **blackguardism:** bad action ● **nasty:** wicked, bad ● **up to:** ready to commit ● **bring the police into it:** call the police for help ● **have a try:** make an attempt ● **on my own:** myself ● **be able to:** succeed in + ing ● **get on their track:** trace them

back out of it: give up, abandon ● **not on my life:** certainly not
bloodthirsty: cruel (taking pleasure in violence and bloodshed)
tearfully: sadly; with tears in her eyes
damned (intensifier) ● **cheek** (fam): arrogance
threatening: menacing
on earth (intensifier used with why? how? when? etc.) ● **go off:** fire
fished out: brought out

whistled: made a noise, letting air through his lips
I'm damned (fam) (excl. of strong surprise) ● **loaded:** equipped with ammunition (bullets) ● **wrapped in thought:** absorbed in thinking
begging: supplicating ● **leave it alone:** drop it

uttered: produced ● **heart-rending:** pitiful ● **sigh** (of distress)
the worst (superlative of bad) ● **the least** (superlative of little)

I feel: my opinion is that

stick together nowadays – they should insist on knowing something about the men they meet.'

'Well?' said George, utterly fogged.

'And the most important thing to a girl is how a man will behave in an emergency – has he got presence of mind – courage – quick-wittedness? That's the kind of thing you can hardly ever know – until it's too late. An emergency mightn't arise until you'd been married for years. All you do know about a man is how he dances and if he's good at getting taxis on a wet night.'

'Both very useful accomplishments,' George pointed out.

'Yes, but one wants to feel a man is a man.'

'The great wide-open spaces where men are men,' George quoted absently.

'Exactly. But we have no wide-open spaces in England. So one has to create a situation artificially. That's what I did.'

'Do you mean –'

'I do mean. That house, as it happens, actually *is* my house. We came to it by design – not by chance. And the man – that man that you nearly killed –'

'Yes?'

'He's Rube Wallace – the film actor. He does prize fighters, you know. The dearest and gentlest of men. I engaged him. Bella's his wife. That's why I was so terrified that you'd killed him. Of course the revolver wasn't loaded. It's a stage property. Oh, George, are you very angry?'

'Am I the first person you have – er – tried this test on?'

'Oh, no. There have been – let me see – nine and a half!'

'Who was the half?' inquired George with curiosity.

'Bingo,' replied Mary coldly.

'Did any of them think of kicking like a mule?'

'No – they didn't. Some tried to bluster and some gave in at once, but they all allowed themselves to be marched upstairs and tied up, and gagged. Then, of course, I managed to work myself loose from my bonds – like in books – and I freed them and we got away – finding the house empty.'

stick together: remain loyal to one another ● **nowadays:** these days ● **meet:** come into contact with
utterly fogged: totally confused (understanding nothing)
<u>to</u> **a girl:** in the eyes of a girl ● **how:** the manner in which
behave: act ● **emergency:** urgency
quick-wittedness: presence of mind (cf line above) ● **kind:** sort
hardly ever: rarely ● **until:** before
mightn't: might not (probability) ● **arise:** happen
<u>do</u> **know** (emphatic) ● **good** <u>at</u> (note the preposition!)
wet: rainy
useful: interesting, advantageous ● **accomplishments:** talents
● **pointed out:** remarked ● **one** (impersonal pronoun)
wide-open spaces: lands of wild nature where man is faced to himself ● **quoted:** recited the quotation (= sentence from a book, a poem or words said by someone else)

as it happens: in fact ● **actually:** in reality
by design: on purpose; ≠ **by chance**
nearly: not quite, almost

prize fighters: boxing matches played for money
the dearest and gentlest (superlatives): the most lovable and non violent ● **wife:** partner in marriage
stage property: theatre accessory
angry: displeased, dissatisfied, irritated
the first: the 1st ● **tried** (verb: to try)
let me see (expression used by s.o who is thinking hard or hesitating) ● **a half:** ½

bluster: boast, show off, pretend they were courageous ● **gave in:** gave up, abandoned ● **allowed:** let
tied up (with a rope) **and gagged** (with a cloth over their mouths) ● **work myself loose:** free myself ● **bonds:** ties (chains or ropes) ● **freed** (verb: to free): released ● **empty:** with nobody in

'And nobody thought of the mule trick or anything like it?'

'No.'

'In that case,' said George graciously, 'I forgive you.'

'Thank you, George,' said Mary meekly.

'In fact,' said George, 'the only question that arises is: Where do we go now? I'm not sure if it's Lambeth Palace or Doctors' Commons, wherever that is.'

'What *are* you talking about?'

'The license. A special license, I think, is indicated. You're too fond of getting engaged to one man and then immediately asking another one to marry you.'

'I didn't ask you to marry me!'

'You did. At Hyde Park Corner. Not a place I should choose for a proposal myself, but everyone has their idiosyncrasies in these matters.'

'I did nothing of the kind. I just asked, as a joke, whether you would care to marry me? It wasn't intended seriously.'

'If I were to take counsel's opinion, I am sure that he would say it constituted a genuine proposal. Besides, you know you want to marry me.'

'I don't.'

'Not after nine and a half failures? Fancy what a feeling of security it will give you to go through life with a man who can extricate you from any dangerous situation.'

Mary appeared to weaken slightly at this telling argument. But she said firmly: 'I wouldn't marry any man unless he went on his knees to me.'

George looked at her. She was adorable. But George had other characteristics of the mule besides its kick. He said with equal firmness:

'To go on one's knees to any woman is degrading. I will not do it.'

Mary said with enchanting wistfulness: 'What a pity!'

They drove back to London. George was stern and silent. Mary's face was hidden by the brim of her hat. As they passed Hyde Park Corner, she murmured softly: 'Couldn't you go on your knees to me?'

trick: technique (of the backward kick!)

graciously: with courtesy and indulgence ● **forgive:** pardon
meekly: gently, humbly
arises: comes to mind
Lambeth Palace: famous historical palace, residence of
the Archbishop of Canterbury (cf p.next page) in London
● **Doctors' Commons:** place where marriages and divorces
were once transacted ● **license:** certificate, permit ● **indicated:**
recommended, required ● **fond of** + ing: inclined to

choose: select ● **a** (marriage) **proposal** ● **everyone** <u>has</u>
(singular) ● **idiosyncrasies:** particular habits ● **matters:**
subjects ● **as a joke:** playfully, not seriously ● **whether:** if
care to: like to
if I were to: if I had to ● **counsel's opinion:** the opinion of a
lawyer ● **genuine:** serious, sincere ● **besides:** what's more

failures ≠ successes ● **fancy:** imagine
go through life: live the experiences of life

weaken: lose her determination ● **slightly:** a little ● **telling:**
significant ● **unless:** except if
went on his knees: knelt down (in supplication)

besides: in addition to
equal firmness: a determination as strong as hers

wistfulness: sadness and regret
stern: very serious, severe, strict
hidden by: not visible under ● **brim:** border

George said firmly: 'No.'

He felt he was being a superman. She admired him for his attitude. But unluckily he suspected her of mulish tendencies herself. He drew up suddenly.

'Excuse me,' he said.

He jumped out of the car, retraced his steps to a fruit barrow they had passed and returned so quickly that the policeman who was bearing down upon them to ask what they meant by it, had not had time to arrive.

George drove on, lightly tossing an apple into Mary's lap.

'Eat more fruit,' he said. 'Also symbolical.'

'Symbolical?'

'Yes, originally Eve gave Adam an apple. Nowadays Adam gives Eve one. See?'

'Yes,' said Mary rather doubtfully.

'Where shall I drive you?' inquired George formally.

'Home, please.'

He drove to Grosvenor Square. His face was absolutely impassive. He jumped out and came round to help her out. She made a last appeal.

'Darling George – couldn't you? Just to please me?'

'Never,' said George.

And at that moment it happened. He slipped, tried to recover his balance and failed. He was kneeling in the mud before her. Mary gave a squeal of joy and clapped her hands.

'Darling George! Now I will marry you. You can go straight to Lambeth Palace and fix up with the Archbishop of Canterbury about it.'

'I didn't mean to,' said George hotly. 'It was a bl – er – a banana skin.' He held the offender up reproachfully.

'Never mind,' said Mary. 'It happened. When we quarrel and you throw it in my teeth that I proposed to you, I can retort that you had to go on your knees to me before I would marry you. And all because of that blessed banana skin! It *was* a blessed banana skin you were going to say?'

'Something of the sort,' said George.

mulish tendencies: tendencies to be as obstinate as a mule
drew up: stood up

retraced his steps: went back ● **fruit barrow:** small cart on wheels in which fruit and vegetables are put to be sold in street markets ● **bearing down upon them:** coming towards them quickly ● **meant by it:** were doing
drove on: continued driving ● **tossing:** throwing
lap: front part of the legs (when seated)

give, **gave**, given

doubtfully: feeling unsure or uncertain
formally: seriously

came round (the car) to her door
last: final ● **appeal:** attempt

never: no way (fam), certainly not
slipped: slid, lost his balance (equilibrium, steadiness)
recover his balance: regain equilibrium ● **failed:** did not succeed ● **mud:** soft wet soil (after rain) ● **squeal:** sharp cry ● **clapped her hands:** applauded

fix up: make arrangements ● **the Archbishop of Canterbury** occupies the highest rank in the hierarchy of the Anglican Church ● **I didn't mean to:** I had no intention to do it ● **bl-:** elliptic for "bloody" ● **offender:** object responsible for the offense (here, the banana skin) ● **never mind:** it doesn't matter, no problem ● **when we quarrel** (future, but not "will" after "when") ● **teeth** or face (here) ● **retort:** reply sharply ● **had to:** were obliged to ● **blessed:** beneficial, opportune ● **it was ... to say:** reference to George's hesitation on the word bl- (cf above)

At five-thirty that afternoon, Mr Leadbetter was informed that his nephew had called and would like to see him.

'Called to eat humble pie,' said Mr Leadbetter to himself. 'I dare say I was rather hard on the lad, but it was for his own good.'

And he gave orders that George should be admitted.

George came in airily.

'I want a few words with you, Uncle,' he said. 'You did me a grave injustice this morning. I should like to know whether, at my age, you could have gone out into the street, disowned by your relatives, and between the hours of eleven-fifteen and five-thirty acquire an income of twenty thousand a year. That is what I have done!'

'You're mad, boy.'

'Not mad; resourceful! I am going to marry a young, rich, beautiful society girl. One, moreover, who is throwing over a duke for my sake.'

'Marrying a girl for her money? I'd not have thought it of you.'

'And you'd have been right. I would never have dared to ask her if she hadn't – very fortunately – asked me. She retracted afterwards, but I made her change her mind. And do you know, Uncle, how all this was done? By a judicious expenditure of twopence and a grasping of the golden ball of opportunity.'

'Why the tuppence?' asked Mr Leadbetter, financially interested.

'One banana – off a barrow. Not everyone would have thought of that banana. Where do you get a marriage license? Is it Doctor's Commons or Lambeth Palace?'

five thirty: 5.30 p.m.

eat humble pie: apologize, excuse himself
I dare say: I must admit ● **hard:** unkind ● **lad** (fam): boy
his own good: emphatic for "his benefit"

airily: in a relaxed and happy manner
a few words: an explanation

disowned: rejected
relatives: family at large ● **eleven-fifteen:** 11.15
five-thirty or half past five ● **income:** wages, salary

mad: crazy, mentally ill, insane
resourceful: good at finding solutions in difficult situations
throwing over: abandoning, giving up

(be) right ≠ (be) wrong ● **dared:** had the courage or impudence
to ● **fortunately:** luckily
change her mind: change her opinion

expenditure (cf verb: to spend money) ● **grasping** (cf verb: to
grasp) ● **the golden ball of opportunity** (reference to the uncle's
words at the beginning of the story) ● **tuppence:** two pence (sing:
penny)

The Thumb Mark of St Peter

Six people who live in a small village have created a club and meet every Tuesday evening to tell each other mysterious crime stories.

The game consists in trying to find the solution to these mysteries.

Among the members of the club are: Miss Marple (A. Christie's famous heroine); Raymond West, her nephew; Joyce Lamprière (she and Raymond are in love with each other); Mr Petherick; Sir Henry Clithering; and Dr Pender.

'And now, Aunt Jane, it is up to you,' said Raymond West.

'Yes, Aunt Jane, we are expecting something really spicy,' chimed in Joyce Lemprière.

'Now, you are laughing at me, my dears,' said Miss Marple placidly. 'You think that because I have lived in this out-of-the-way spot all my life I am not likely to have had any very interesting experiences.'

'God forbid that I should ever regard village life as peaceful and uneventful,' said Raymond with fervour. 'Not after the horrible revelations we have heard from you! The cosmopolitan world seems a mild and peaceful place compared with St Mary Mead.'

'Well, my dear,' said Miss Marple, 'human nature is much the same everywhere, and, of course, one has opportunities of observing it at close quarters in a village.'

'You really are unique, Aunt Jane,' cried Joyce. 'I hope you don't mind me calling you Aunt Jane?' she added. 'I don't know why I do it.'

'Don't you, my dear?' said Miss Marple.

She looked up for a moment or two with something quizzical in her glance, which made the blood flame to the

thumb: first digit of the hand

aunt, uncle; nephew, niece ● **it's up to you:** it's your turn

expecting: anticipating, hoping for ● **spicy:** sensational
chimed in: echoed
laughing <u>at</u> me: mocking me ● **dears** (affectionate term)
placidly: calmly ● **out-of the-way:** distant and unfrequented
spot: place, geographical area ● **all my life:** since birth ● **I am
not likely to have had:** I probably haven't had
God forbid: expression of protest ● **regard:** consider
peaceful: tranquil, calm ● **uneventful:** where no incident
happens ● **heard <u>from</u>** (note the preposition!)
cosmopolitan: urban ● **seems:** appears to be ● **mild:** quiet

much the same: very similar ● **one:** impersonal pronoun
opportunities: occasions, chances
at close quarters: precisely, with attention
unique: remarkable ● **cried:** exclaimed
you don't mind: you have no objection to ● **calling you** by the
name of... ● **I don't know:** I have no idea
Don't you ...?: ironical allusion to Joyce and Raymond's love
story
quizzical: questioning and mocking ● **glance:** look ● **which**

girl's cheeks. Raymond West fidgeted and cleared his throat in a somewhat embarrassed manner.

Miss Marple looked at them both and smiled again, and bent her attention once more to her knitting.

'It is true, of course, that I have lived what is called a very uneventful life, but I have had a lot of experience in solving different little problems that have arisen. Some of them have been really quite ingenious; but it would be no good telling them to you, because they are about such unimportant things that you would not be interested – just things like: Who cut the meshes of Mrs Jones's string bag? and why Mrs Sims only wore her new fur coat once. Very interesting things, really, to any student of human nature. No, the only experience I can remember that would be of interest to you is the one about my poor niece Mabel's husband.

'It is about ten or fifteen years ago now, and happily it is all over and done with, and everyone has forgotten about it. People's memories are very short – a lucky thing, I always think.'

Miss Marple paused and murmured to herself:

'I must just count this row. The decreasing is a little awkward. One, two, three, four, five, and then three purl; that is right. Now, what was I saying? Oh, yes, about poor Mabel.

'Mabel was my niece. A nice girl, really a very nice girl, but just a trifle what one might call silly. Rather fond of being melodramatic and of saying a great deal more than she meant whenever she was upset. She married a Mr Denman when she was twenty-two, and I am afraid it was not a very happy marriage. I had hoped very much that the attachment would not come to anything, for Mr Denman was a man of very violent temper – not the kind of man who would be patient with Mabel's foibles – and I also learned that there was insanity in his family. However, girls were just as obstinate then as they are now, and as they always will be. And Mabel married him.

'I didn't see very much of her after her marriage. She came to stay with me once or twice, and they asked me there

made... cheeks (Joyce's face went red with embarrassment)
● **fidgeted:** made small nervous movements ● **cleared his throat,**
producing a "hem, h'm" sound ● **them both:** the two of them
● **smiled:** showed amusement on her face ● **bent:** concentrated
● **knitting:** activity consisting in making a piece of clothing
with wool and two needles ● **true:** exact ● **solving:** finding
the solution to ● arise, arose, **arisen:** happened, taken place,
occurred ● **ingenious:** intelligent ● **it would be no good** + ing:
there is no interest in + ing
cut, **cut,** cut (with scissors)
meshes: *mailles d'un filet* ● **string:** cord
wear, **wore,** worn (clothes) ● **fur:** animal hairs ● **once:** on one
occasion ● a **student** studies a subject (at school, university)

poor: adj. expressing pity ● **husband:** woman's partner in
marriage ● **ago:** before ● **happily:** luckily
all over and done with: finished ● **everyone has forgotten:**
nobody remembers ● **short** ≠ long ● **a lucky thing:** a good
thing

count one, two, three ... ● **row:** line ● **decreasing:** diminishing
awkward: difficult ● **purl:** *point à l'envers*
right: correct (≠ wrong)

nice: kind, good
a trifle: a little ● **silly:** stupid ● **fond of** + ing: inclined to
saying ... she meant (mean, **meant,** meant: signify):
exaggerating ● **whenever:** on any occasion ● **upset:**
emotionally distressed, confused ● **I am afraid:** I am sorry to say
hoped: wished, wanted
come to anything: result in a serious union
temper: character ● **kind:** sort
foibles: imperfections, defects ● **learned** (or learnt): got to know
insanity: disorder of the mind, madness ● **however**
(contradiction) ● **then** (in the past) **now** (at present) **always** (in
the future)
I didn't see ... her: I lost contact with her
stay: reside temporarily ● **once or twice:** on one or two occasions

several times, but, as a matter of fact, I am not very fond of staying in other people's houses, and I always managed to make some excuse. They had been married ten years when Mr Denman died suddenly. There were no children, and he left all his money to Mabel. I wrote, of course, and offered to come to Mabel if she wanted me; but she wrote back a very sensible letter, and I gathered that she was not altogether overwhelmed by grief. I thought that was only natural, because I knew they had not been getting on together for some time. It was not until about three months afterwards that I got a most hysterical letter from Mabel, begging me to come to her, and saying that things were going from bad to worse, and she couldn't stand it much longer.

'So, of course,' continued Miss Marple, 'I put Clara on board wages and sent the plate and the King Charles tankard to the bank, and I went off at once. I found Mabel in a very nervous state. The house, Myrtle Dene, was a fairly large one, very comfortably furnished. There was a cook and a house-parlourmaid as well as a nurse-attendant to look after old Mr Denman, Mabel's husband's father, who was what is called "not quite right in the head". Quite peaceful and well-behaved, but distinctly odd at times. As I say, there was insanity in the family.

'I was really shocked to see the change in Mabel. She was a mass of nerves, twitching all over, yet I had the greatest difficulty in making her tell me what the trouble was. I got at it, as one always does get at these things, indirectly. I asked her about some friends of hers she was always mentioning in her letters, the Gallaghers. She said, to my surprise, that she hardly ever saw them nowadays. Other friends whom I mentioned elicited the same remark. I spoke to her then of the folly of shutting herself up and brooding, and especially of the silliness of cutting herself adrift from her friends. Then she came bursting out with the truth.

'"It is not my doing, it is theirs. There is not a soul in the place who will speak to me now. When I go down the High Street they all get out of the way so that they shan't have to meet me or speak to me. I am like a kind of leper. It is

several times: on many occasions ● **as a matter of fact:** in
fact, in reality ● **managed:** had success in, succeeded in + ing

died: ceased to live, to exist ● **children:** descendants
left: donated ● **money:** fortune ● write, **wrote,** written (a letter)
wanted: needed ● **sensible:** full of common sense (good
judgement) ● **gathered:** concluded ● **not altogether ... grief:**
not totally distressed by her husband's death
getting on together: having a harmonious relationship
some time: a certain time ● **afterwards:** later
most: extremely ● **begging:** supplicating
going from bad to worse: deteriorating
she couldn't stand it: it was impossible for her to face the
situation; to stand: to bear
on board wages: on a reduced salary ● **sent ... to the bank:**
put all my precious objects to be kept in a bank ● **went off** (to
see her) ● **at once:** immediately ● **state** (of mind): mood
● **fairly large:** quite big ● **furnished** with tables, chairs,
wardrobes, etc. ● a **cook** prepares the meals in the kitchen
parlourmaid: female servant ● **nurse-attendant:** woman who
looks after (is in charge of) an old or sick person ● **not quite
right in the head:** mentally deranged ● **well behaved:** correct
● **odd:** strange, bizarre

twitching: having nervous muscular spasms **all over** her body
trouble: problem ● **got at it:** finally had the answer
one (impersonal pronoun)
friends of <u>hers</u> (possessive pronoun: mine, yours, etc.)
the Gallagher<u>s</u>: note the plural!
hardly ever: very rarely ● **now(adays):** these days
elicited: produced ● **the same remark:** a similar comment
shutting herself up: confining herself ● **brooding:** having
morbid ideas ● **silliness:** stupidity ● **adrift:** apart
bursting ... the truth: suddenly telling what the problem really
was ● **it is not my doing:** I am not responsible for it ● **not a soul:**
nobody ● **High Street:** main, principal street ● **get out of the
way:** change direction ● **shan't have to:** won't be obliged to
kind: sort ● a **leper** suffers from leprosy (an infectious disease)

awful, and I can't bear it any longer. I shall have to sell the house and go abroad. Yet why should I be driven away from a home like this? I have done nothing."

'I was more disturbed than I can tell you. I was knitting a comforter for old Mrs Hay at the time, and in my perturbation I dropped two stitches and never discovered it until long after.

' "My dear Mabel," I said, "you amaze me. But what is the cause of all this?"

'Even as a child Mabel was always difficult. I had the greatest difficulty in getting her to give me a straightforward answer to my question. She would only say vague things about wicked talk and idle people who had nothing better to do than gossip, and people who put ideas into other people's heads.

' "That is all quite clear to me," I said. "There is evidently some story being circulated about you. But what that story is you must know as well as anyone. And you are going to tell me."

' "It is so wicked," moaned Mabel.

' "Of course it is wicked," I said briskly. "There is nothing that you can tell me about people's minds that would astonish or surprise me. Now, Mabel, will you tell me in plain English what people are saying about you?"

'Then it all came out.

'It seemed that Geoffrey Denman's death, being quite sudden and unexpected, gave rise to various rumours. In fact – and in plain English as I had put it to her – people were saying that she had poisoned her husband.

'Now, as I expect you know, there is nothing more cruel than talk, and there is nothing more difficult to combat. When people say things behind your back there is nothing you can refute or deny, and the rumours go on growing and growing, and no one can stop them. I was quite certain of one thing: Mabel was quite incapable of poisoning anyone. And I didn't see why life should be ruined for her and her home made unbearable just because in all probability she had been doing something silly and foolish.

I can't bear it: it's impossible for me to face the situation
abroad: to a foreign country • **driven away from:** forced to leave
disturbed: perturbed
comforter: woollen scarf worn around the neck
dropped: missed • **stitches** (stitch: *maille de tricot*)

amaze: stupefy

straightforward: direct
would (indicates a past habit)
wicked talk: malicious rumours • **idle:** unoccupied, inactive
gossip: have malicious conversations about other people

wicked: malevolent • **moaned:** said with a complaining voice
briskly: abruptly
minds: mentalities
plain English: simple, understandable language

it all came out: she told the complete story

unexpected: surprising • **gave rise to:** caused, produced

I expect: I suppose
combat: fight against
behind your back: secretly, without you knowing it
deny: say it's false • **growing and growing:** getting more and more important

ruined: destroyed
unbearable: impossible to endure or bear
silly, foolish: stupid, unwise, absurd

'"There is no smoke without fire," I said. "Now, Mabel, you have got to tell me what started people off on this track. There must have been something."

'Mabel was very incoherent, and declared there was nothing – nothing at all, except, of course, that Geoffrey's death had been very sudden. He had seemed quite well at supper that evening, and was taken violently ill in the night. The doctor had been sent for, but the poor man had died a few minutes after the doctor's arrival. Death had been thought to be the result of eating poisoned mushrooms.

'"Well," I said, "I suppose a sudden death of that kind might start tongues wagging, but surely not without some additional facts. Did you have a quarrel with Geoffrey or anything of that kind?"

'She admitted that she had had a quarrel with him on the preceding morning at breakfast time.

'"And the servants heard it, I suppose?" I asked.

'"They weren't in the room."

'"No, my dear," I said, "but they probably were fairly near the door outside."

'I knew the carrying power of Mabel's high-pitched hysterical voice only too well. Geoffrey Denman, too, was a man given to raising his voice loudly when angry.

'"What did you quarrel about?" I asked.

'"Oh, the usual things. It was always the same things over and over again. Some little thing would start us off, and then Geoffrey became impossible and said abominable things, and I told him what I thought of him."

'"There had been a lot of quarrelling, then?" I asked.

'"It wasn't my fault –"

'"My dear child," I said, "it doesn't matter whose fault it was. That is not what we are discussing. In a place like this everybody's private affairs are more or less public property. You and your husband were always quarrelling. You had a particularly bad quarrel one morning, and that night your husband died suddenly and mysteriously. Is that all, or is there anything else?"

There is no smoke without fire (proverb): every rumour is based on a real fact ● **what ... on this track:** what made people think that way ● **must** expresses a certainty

death (noun); to die (verb) ● **quite well:** in good health, not ill
supper: evening meal ● **was taken:** had become ● **ill:** unwell, in bad health ● **had been sent for** (passive form): had been called
amanita are poisonous **mushrooms,** but boletus is edible!

start tongues wagging: cause gossiping (cf previous page, gossip); **tongue:** organ used when speaking ● **quarrel:** disagreement, argument
had had (past perfect or pluperfect)
preceding morning: previous morning, morning before
hear, **heard,** heard

fairly near: quite near, not far from
outside ≠ inside
carrying power: capacity to be heard from a distance ● **high-pitched:** high in tone ≠ low ● **only too** (intensifier): very
given to: apt to ● **raising** (the volume of) **his voice** ● **angry:** dissatisfied
usual: habitual ● **over and over again:** repeatedly
start us off: be at the origin of the quarrel
become, **became,** become (idea of evolution) ● say, **said,** said
tell, **told,** told ● think, **thought,** thought

it doesn't matter: it makes no difference

more or less: to a great degree ● **public property:** sthg that belongs to everybody

all: everything
anything else: another fact or detail

' "I don't know what you mean by anything else," said Mabel sullenly.

' "Just what I say, my dear. If you have done anything silly, don't for Heaven's sake keep it back now. I only want to do what I can to help you."

' "Nothing and nobody can help me," said Mabel wildly, "except death."

' "Have a little more faith in Providence, dear," I said. "Now then, Mabel, I know perfectly well there is something else that you are keeping back."

'I always did know, even when she was a child, when she was not telling me the whole truth. It took a long time, but I got it out at last. She had gone down to the chemist's that morning and had bought some arsenic. She had had, of course, to sign the book for it. Naturally, the chemist had talked.

' "Who is your doctor?" I asked.

' "Dr Rawlinson."

'I knew him by sight. Mabel had pointed him out to me the other day. To put it in perfectly plain language he was what I would describe as an old dodderer. I have had too much experience of life to believe in the infallibility of doctors. Some of them are clever men and some of them are not, and half the time the best of them don't know what is the matter with you. I have no truck with doctors and their medicines myself.

'I thought things over, and then I put my bonnet on and went to call on Dr Rawlinson. He was just what I had thought him – a nice old man, kindly, vague, and so short-sighted as to be pitiful, slightly deaf, and, withal, touchy and sensitive to the last degree. He was on his high horse at once when I mentioned Geoffrey Denman's death, talked for a long time about various kinds of fungi, edible and otherwise. He had questioned the cook, and she had admitted that one or two of the mushrooms cooked had been "a little queer", but as the shop had sent them she thought they must be all right. The more she had thought about them since, the more she was convinced that their appearance was unusual.

mean: are suggesting
sullenly: with morosity or sadness
just: exactly
for Heaven's sake (excl. of impatience) ● **keep it back:** keep it
secret ● **help:** assist
wildly: without self-control

faith: confidence ● **Providence:** destiny

<u>**did**</u> **know** (emphatic form)**:** knew
whole: complete ● **the truth:** the real story
I got it out (from her mouth!) ● **at last:** finally ● **the chemist's**
(shop) is where you buy (bought, **bought**) medicine ● **had had**
to: had been obliged to ● **book:** register

by sight: not personally ● **pointed (him) out:** indicated by
pointing her finger ● **to put it ... plain language:** to be explicit
old dodderer: person who hesitates and trembles because of
old age
clever: capable, competent
half: 50 % ● **the best** (superlative form of good) ● **matter:**
problem ● **I have no truck with:** I don't want any connection
with
thought things over: reflected on the subject ● **bonnet:** old
type of hat ● **what I had thought him:** like I had imagined him
nice, kindly: amiable ● **short-sighted:** suffering from myopia
slightly: a little ● **deaf:** who can't hear ● **withal:** also ● **touchy**
and sensitive to the last degree: very easily affected ● **on his**
high horse: irritated
fungi or mushrooms can be **edible** or poisonous
the cook prepares (or cooks) the meals in the kitchen
queer: strange, not normal
send, **sent,** sent: delivered
the more ... the more (expresses a progression)
convinced: sure, certain ● **unusual:** not normal

' "She would be," I said. "They would start by being quite like mushrooms in appearance, and they would end by being orange with purple spots. There is nothing that class cannot remember if it tries."

'I gathered that Denman had been past speech when the doctor got to him. He was incapable of swallowing, and had died within a few minutes. The doctor seemed perfectly satisfied with the certificate he had given. But how much of that was obstinacy and how much of it was genuine belief I could not be sure.

'I went straight home and asked Mabel quite frankly why she had bought arsenic.

' "You must have had some idea in your mind," I pointed out.

'Mabel burst into tears. "I wanted to make away with myself," she moaned. "I was too unhappy. I thought I would end it all."

' "Have you the arsenic still?" I asked.

' "No, I threw it away."

'I sat there turning things over and over in my mind.

' "What happened when he was taken ill? Did he call you?"

' "No." She shook her head. "He rang the bell violently. He must have rung several times. At last Dorothy, the house-parlourmaid, heard it, and she waked the cook up, and they came down. When Dorothy saw him she was frightened. He was rambling and delirious. She left the cook with him and came rushing to me. I got up and went to him. Of course I saw at once he was dreadfully ill. Unfortunately Brewster, who looks after old Mr Denman, was away for the night, so there was no one who knew what to do. I sent Dorothy off for the doctor, and the cook and I stayed with him, but after a few minutes I couldn't bear it any longer; it was too dreadful. I ran away back to my room and locked the door."

' "Very selfish and unkind of you," I said; "and no doubt that conduct of yours has done nothing to help you since, you may be sure of that. The cook will have repeated it everywhere. Well, well, this is a bad business."

she would be: of course she was
end: finish ≠ start, begin
purple: mixture of blue and red ● **spots:** marks ● (social) **class**
tries (cf try: make efforts)
gathered: deduced ● **past speech:** unable to speak
swallowing: absorbing food or drink

satisfied <u>with</u> (note the preposition!)
obstinacy: stubbornness ● **genuine:** sincere ● **belief:**
conviction
straight: immediately

you must have had: you certainly had ● **mind:** head ● **pointed
out:** remarked
burst, **burst,** burst **into tears:** started crying ● **make away with
myself:** commit suicide ● **moaned:** said plaintively ● **too** + adj:
excessively ● **end:** finish
still: adverb expressing continuation
throw, **threw,** thrown **it away:** didn't keep it
over and over: repeatedly
was taken ill (note the passive form!): became ill (= unwell)

shake, **shook,** shaken **her head** (meaning "no") ● ring, **rang,**
rung
waked (or woke) **up** (from sleep)
frightened: alarmed, panicked
rambling: speaking nonsense ● leave, **left,** left
came rushing: arrived very quickly ● get, **got,** got **up** (from
bed) ● **dreadfully:** terribly ● **unfortunately:** unluckily (adv.
expressing regret) ● **away:** absent
know, **knew,** known ● send, **sent,** sent **Dorothy off for:** asked
Dorothy to go and get or to fetch
a few: some ● **I couldn't bear it:** it was impossible for me to
face the situation ● **ran away:** escaped ● **locked** (with a key)
selfish and unkind: inconsiderate towards the others
that conduct of yours (of mine, of his, of hers, etc.): your
attitude
bad ≠ good ● **business:** matter, case

'Next I spoke to the servants. The cook wanted to tell me about the mushrooms, but I stopped her. I was tired of these mushrooms. Instead, I questioned both of them very closely about their master's condition on that night. They both agreed that he seemed to be in great agony, that he was unable to swallow, and he could only speak in a strangled voice, and when he did speak it was only rambling – nothing sensible.

'"What did he say when he was rambling?" I asked curiously.

'"Something about some fish, wasn't it?" turning to the other.

'Dorothy agreed.

'"A heap of fish," she said; "some nonsense like that. I could see at once he wasn't in his right mind, poor gentleman."

'There didn't seem to be any sense to be made out of that. As a last resource I went up to see Brewster, who was a gaunt, middle-aged woman of about fifty.

'"It is a pity that I wasn't here that night," she said. "Nobody seems to have tried to do anything for him until the doctor came."

'"I suppose he was delirious," I said doubtfully; "but that is not a symptom of ptomaine poisoning, is it?"

'"It depends," said Brewster.

'I asked her how her patient was getting on.

'She shook her head.

'"He is pretty bad," she said.

'"Weak?"

'"Oh no, he is strong enough physically – all but his eyesight. That is failing badly. He may outlive all of us, but his mind is failing very fast now. I have already told both Mr and Mrs Denman that he ought to be in an institution, but Mrs Denman wouldn't hear of it at any price."

'I will say for Mabel that she always had a kindly heart.

'Well, there the thing was. I thought it over in every aspect, and at last I decided that there was only one thing to be done. In view of the rumours that were going about, permission must be applied for to exhume the body, and a proper post-mortem must be made and lying tongues quietened once and

speak, **spoke,** spoken
I was tired of: I had heard enough about
instead: as an alternative ● **closely:** precisely
condition: state of health ● **agreed:** said the same thing
unable to: incapable of + ing
strangled: not clear
<u>**did**</u> **speak** (emphatic form): spoke ● **sensible:** that makes
sense, judicious

agreed: gave confirmation
heap: great quantity, pile
not in his right mind: not mentally sane

resource: solution ● **gaunt:** emaciated and haggard
middle-aged (characteristic): around **fifty** (50) years old
it is a pity (expression of regret)
tried: attempted ● **until:** before

ptomaine poisoning: food poisoning

getting on: progressing physically
shake, **shook,** shaken **her head:** moved her head
pretty + adj (intensifier): quite, very
weak: feeble ; ≠ strong
strong: robust; healthy; ≠ weak ● **but:** except ● **eyesight:** vision
failing: deteriorating ● **outlive:** live longer than
fast: quickly, rapidly
ought to: should ● **institution:** hospital
would't: didn't want to ● **at any price:** on any condition, (not) at
all ● **for:** in favour of ● **a kindly heart:** a generous attitude
the thing: the question ● **thought it over:** reflected about it
at last: finally ● **in view of:** because of ● **going about:**
spreading ● **applied for:** asked for ● **proper:** serious ● **post-
mortem:** legal medical examination of a dead body ● **lying
tongues:** defamatory gossips ● **quietened:** reduced to silence

for all. Mabel, of course, made a fuss, mostly on sentimental grounds – disturbing the dead man in his peaceful grave, etc., etc. – but I was firm.

'I won't make a long story of this part of it. We got the order and they did the autopsy, or whatever they call it, but the result was not so satisfactory as it might have been. There was no trace of arsenic – that was all to the good – but the actual words of the report were *that there was nothing to show by what means deceased had come to his death*.

'So, you see, that didn't lead us out of trouble altogether. People went on talking – about rare poisons impossible to detect, and rubbish of that sort. I had seen the pathologist who had done the post-mortem, and I had asked him several questions, though he tried his best to get out of answering most of them; but I got out of him that he considered it highly unlikely that the poisoned mushrooms were the cause of death. An idea was simmering in my mind, and I asked him what poison, if any, could have been employed to obtain that result. He made a long explanation to me, most of which, I must admit, I did not follow, but it amounted to this: That death might have been due to some strong vegetable alkaloid.

'The idea I had was this: Supposing the taint of insanity was in Geoffrey Denman's blood also, might he not have made away with himself? He had, at one period of his life, studied medicine, and he would have a good knowledge of poisons and their effects.

'I didn't think it sounded very likely, but it was the only thing I could think of. And I was nearly at my wits' end, I can tell you. Now, I dare say you modern young people will laugh, but when I am in really bad trouble I always say a little prayer to myself – anywhere, when I am walking along the street, or at a bazaar. And I always get an answer. It may be some trifling thing, apparently quite unconnected with the subject, but there it is. I had that text pinned over my bed when I was a little girl: *Ask and you shall receive*. On the morning that I am telling you about, I was walking along the High Street, and I was praying hard. I shut my eyes, and

(once) for all: forever ● **a fuss:** a scandal ● **mostly:** principally
on ... grounds: for ... reasons ● **disturbing:** breaking the peace
● **grave:** tomb ● **firm:** determined

order: permission

all to the good: a good thing ● **actual:** exact

show: prove ● **by what means:** how ● **deceased** (formal): dead
that didn't ... altogether: it wasn't the end of our problems at all
go, **went,** gone **on** + ing: continued
rubbish (sing): nonsense (sing) ● **pathologist:** doctor who is a
specialist of diseases **several:** a series of
(al)though: even if ● **tried his best:** made efforts ● **get out of:**
avoid ● **most:** the majority ● **got out of him:** managed to make
him say ● **highly:** very ● **unlikely:** improbable
simmering: germinating
employed: used
explanation (noun); explain (verb)
follow: understand ● **amounted:** was equivalent to
vegetable: derived from a plant

blood flows in the veins

knowledge (noun); know, knew, known (verb)

likely: probable
at my wits' end: not knowing what to do
I dare say: I suppose
laugh: be amused
prayer: question or supplication often addressed to God

trifling: unimportant ● **unconnected:** without any relation to
pinned (on the wall) **over my bed**
shall (emphatic form of "will")
High Street: main street ● **hard:** with concentration ● shut,
shut, shut: closed

when I opened them, what do you think was the first thing that I saw?'

Five faces with varying degrees of interest were turned to Miss Marple. It may be safely assumed, however, that no one would have guessed the answer to the question right.

'I saw,' said Miss Marple impressively, '*the window of the fishmonger's shop*. There was only one thing in it, *a fresh haddock*.'

She looked round triumphantly.

'Oh, my God!' said Raymond West. 'An answer to prayer – a fresh haddock!'

'Yes, Raymond,' said Miss Marple severely, 'and there is no need to be profane about it. The hand of God is everywhere. The first thing I saw were the black spots – the marks of St Peter's thumb. That is the legend, you know. St Peter's thumb. And that brought things home to me. I needed faith, the ever true faith of St Peter. I connected the two things together, faith – and fish.'

Sir Henry blew his nose rather hurriedly. Joyce bit her lip.

'Now what did that bring to my mind? Of course, both the cook and house-parlourmaid mentioned fish as being one of the things spoken of by the dying man. I was convinced, absolutely convinced, that there was some solution of the mystery to be found in these words. I went home determined to get to the bottom of the matter.'

She paused.

'Has it ever occurred to you,' the old lady went on, 'how much we go by what is called, I believe, the context? There is a place on Dartmoor called Grey Wethers. If you were talking to a farmer there and mentioned Grey Wethers, he would probably conclude that you were speaking of these stone circles, yet it is possible that you might be speaking of the atmosphere; and in the same way, if you were meaning the stone circles, an outsider, hearing a fragment of the conversation, might think you meant the weather. So when we repeat a conversation, we don't, as a rule, repeat the actual words; we put in some other words that seem to us to mean exactly the same thing.

see, **saw**, seen

it may be safely assumed: we can be quite sure; there is little doubt ● **guessed the answer right:** found the right (= correct) answer ● **(shop)window:** where the things for sale are displayed ● **fresh:** just out of the water
haddock: common fish found in Northern seas
round: all around her

profane: disrespectful, blasphemous

brought things home to me: made me understand everything
ever: always ● **true:** sincere

blow, **blew,** blown **his nose** ● bite, **bit,** bitten (with the teeth) ● **lip:** the upper lip and the lower lip (around the mouth)

spoken of: mentioned ● **dying:** agonizing

be found (passive form)
get to the bottom of the matter: understand everything

occurred to you: come to your mind ● **went on:** continued
go by: form our opinion on
Dartmoor: moorland in South West England (Devon county)

stone (adj): piece of rock ● **yet** (contrast)
meaning: having in mind
outsider: someone who does not take part in the conversation
weather: climatic conditions ● **so:** consequently
as a rule: usually, generally ● **actual:** exact
mean, meant, meant: signify, represent

'I saw both the cook and Dorothy separately. I asked the cook if she was quite sure that her master had really mentioned a heap of fish. She said she was quite sure.

' "Were these his exact words," I asked, "or did he mention some particular kind of fish?"

' "That's it," said the cook; "it was some particular kind of fish, but I can't remember what now. A heap of – now what was it? Not any of the fish you send to table. Would it be a perch now – or pike? No. It didn't begin with a P."

'Dorothy also recalled that her master had mentioned some special kind of fish. "Some outlandish kind of fish it was," she said.

' "A pile of – now what was it?"

' "Did he say heap or pile?" I asked.

' "I think he said pile. But there, I really can't be sure – it's so hard to remember the actual words, isn't it, Miss, especially when they don't seem to make sense. But now I come to think of it, I am pretty sure that it was a pile, and the fish began with C; but it wasn't a cod or a crayfish."

'The next part is where I am really proud of myself,' said Miss Marple, 'because, of course, I don't know anything about drugs – nasty, dangerous things I call them. I have got an old recipe of my grandmother's for tansy tea that is worth any amount of your drugs. But I knew that there were several medical volumes in the house, and in one of them there was an index of drugs. You see, my idea was that Geoffrey had taken some particular poison, and was trying to say the name of it.

'Well, I looked down the list of H's, beginning He. Nothing there that sounded likely; then I began on the P's, and almost at once I came to – what do you think?'

She looked round, postponing her moment of triumph.

'Pilocarpine. Can't you understand a man who could hardly speak trying to drag that word out? What would that sound like to a cook who had never heard the word? Wouldn't it convey the impression "pile of carp?" '

'By Jove!' said Sir Henry.

'I should never have hit upon that,' said Dr Pender.

quite: absolutely

kind: sort

you send to table: that are commonly eaten
perch; pike: types of fish that live in rivers or lakes
recalled: remembered
outlandish: not common, exotic

heap and **pile** are synonyms

hard: difficult • **actual:** real, exact
now I come to think of it: in fact
pretty + adj (intensifier): quite
begin, **began,** begun: started • **cod:** type of sea-fish
crayfish: *écrevisse* • **proud of:** satisfied with

drugs: chemical products used as medicine • **nasty:** bad,
dangerous • **recipe:** instructions for preparing • **tansy tea:**
infusion of a plant supposed to prolong life • **is worth:** has the
same quality as • **amount:** quantity • **several:** more than one;
a few • **volumes:** books, dictionaries • **index:** alphabetical list
taken: absorbed, swallowed
say: pronounce

postponing: delaying, putting off to later
could hardly speak: had great difficulties in speaking
drag out: say with great difficulty

convey: give
By Jove! (old-fashion) exclamation of surprise and admiration
hit upon that: have enough perspicacity to find that

'Most interesting,' said Mr Petherick. 'Really most interesting.'

'I turned quickly to the page indicated in the index. I read about pilocarpine and its effect on the eyes and other things that didn't seem to have any bearing on the case, but at last I came to a most significant phrase: *Has been tried with success as an antidote for atropine poisoning.*

'I can't tell you the light that dawned upon me then. I never had thought it likely that Geoffrey Denman would commit suicide. No, this new solution was not only possible, but I was absolutely sure it was the correct one, because all the pieces fitted in logically.'

'I am not going to try to guess,' said Raymond. 'Go on, Aunt Jane, and tell us what was so startlingly clear to you.'

'I don't know anything about medicine, of course,' said Miss Marple, 'but I did happen to know this, that when my eyesight was failing, the doctor ordered me drops with atropine sulphate in them. I went straight upstairs to old Mr Denman's room. I didn't beat about the bush.

'"Mr Denman," I said, "I know everything. Why did you poison your son?"

'He looked at me for a minute or two – rather a handsome old man he was, in his way – and then he burst out laughing. It was one of the most vicious laughs I have ever heard. I can assure you it made my flesh creep. I had only heard anything like it once before, when poor Mrs Jones went off her head.

'"Yes," he said, "I got even with Geoffrey. I was too clever for Geoffrey. He was going to put me away, was he? Have me shut up in an asylum? I heard them talking about it. Mabel is a good girl – Mabel stuck up for me, but I knew she wouldn't be able to stand up against Geoffrey. In the end he would have his own way; he always did. But I settled him – I settled my kind, loving son! Ha, ha! I crept down in the night. It was quite easy. Brewster was away. My dear son was asleep; he had a glass of water by the side of his bed; he always woke up in the middle of the night and drank it off. I poured it away – ha, ha! – and I emptied the bottle of eyedrops into the glass. He would wake up and swill it down before he knew

most: extremely

bearing on: connection with
significant: meaningful, enlightening ● **tried:** experimented

the light that dawned upon me: how everything became
suddenly clear to me

fitted in: corresponded (like the pieces of a puzzle)

startingly: surprisingly

<u>did</u> **happen to know** (emphatic): knew
eyesight: vision ● **failing:** deteriorating ● **ordered:** prescribed
● **drops:** liquid medicine ● **upstairs:** (to the bedroom);
≠ downstairs ● **I didn't beat about the bush:** I went straight
(directly) to the point
son: male child
rather: quite ● **handsome:** elegant
burst out laughing: suddenly started to laugh (express
amusement or incredulity noisily)
made my flesh creep: made me shiver (tremble) with shock
went off her head: became insane, crazy, mad
got even with: had my revenge upon ● **clever:** intelligent
away (from home)
shut up: confined (as if in prison) ● (lunatic) **asylum:** mental home
stick, **stuck,** stuck **up for me:** supported me, defended me
able to: capable of + ing ● **stand up against:** resist ● **in the end:**
finally ● **his own way:** what he wanted ● **settled:** disposed, got rid of
● **kind, loving** (ironical, here!) ● creep, **crept,** crept **down:** went
down the stairs quietly ● **easy** ≠ difficult ● **asleep** (adj): sleeping
by the side (left or right) **of:** next to, near ● **woke up** (cf wake
up) ● **drank** (cf drink) ● **off:** completely ● **poured it away:**
threw it away ● **emptied:** poured ● **eyedrops:** liquid medicine
for ophtalmic problems ● **swill it down:** swallow it; drink it up

what it was. There was only a tablespoonful of it – quite enough, quite enough. And so he did! They came to me in the morning and broke it to me very gently. They were afraid it would upset me. Ha! Ha! Ha! Ha! Ha!"

'Well,' said Miss Marple, 'that is the end of the story. Of course, the poor old man was put in an asylum. He wasn't really responsible for what he had done, and the truth was known, and everyone was sorry for Mabel and could not do enough to make up to her for the unjust suspicions they had had. But if it hadn't been for Geoffrey realizing what the stuff was he had swallowed and trying to get everybody to get hold of the antidote without delay, it might never have been found out. I believe there are very definite symptoms with atropine – dilated pupils of the eyes, and all that; but, of course, as I have said, Dr Rawlinson was very shortsighted, poor old man. And in the same medical book which I went on reading – and some of it was *most* interesting – it gave the symptoms of ptomaine poisoning and atropine, and they are not unlike. But I can assure you I have never seen a pile of fresh haddock without thinking of the thumb mark of St Peter.'

There was a very long pause.

'My dear friend,' said Mr Petherick. 'My very dear friend, you really are amazing.'

'I shall recommend Scotland Yard to come to you for advice,' said Sir Henry.

'Well, at all events, Aunt Jane,' said Raymond, 'there is one thing that you don't know.'

'Oh, yes, I do, dear,' said Miss Marple. 'It happened just before dinner, didn't it? When you took Joyce out to admire the sunset. It is a very favourite place, that. There by the jasmine hedge. That is where the milkman asked Annie if he could put up the banns.'

'Dash it all, Aunt Jane,' said Raymond, 'don't spoil all the romance. Joyce and I aren't like the milkman and Annie.'

'That is where you make a mistake, dear,' said Miss Marple. 'Everybody is very much alike, really. But fortunately, perhaps, they don't realize it.'

tablespoonful: measure equivalent to the contents of a
tablespoon ● **enough:** sufficient ● **so he did!:** that's what he did
broke it to me: told me the news
upset me: make me feel sad

responsible <u>for</u> (note the preposition!) ● **truth:** true (= real)
story ● **was known** (passive form): became public ● **was sorry:**
felt pity ● **make up for**: excuse themselves ● **unjust:** unfair
if ... realizing: if Geoffrey hadn't realized ● **stuff:** thing
get hold of: find
without delay: quickly ● **found out:** discovered
definite: clear, precise

went on + ing: continued + ing
most + adj (intensifier): extremely
not unlike: similar

amazing: extraordinary, wonderful
Scotland Yard: division of the London police dealing with
criminal affairs ● **advice** (sing): counselling
at all events: in any case

sunset: sun disappearing below the horizon ≠ sunrise
hedge: row of plants ● the **milkman** delivers milk at people's
doors ● **put up the banns:** officially declare his intention to
marry her ● **dash it all** (excl. of protest): damn it (fam.) ● **spoil:**
damage the beauty of ● **romance:** love story ● **Joyce and <u>I</u>**; not
"me" (subject) ● **mistake:** error
alike: similar ● **fortunately:** luckily; it's a good thing

The Witness for the Prosecution

Mr Mayherne adjusted his pince-nez and cleared his throat with a little dry-as-dust cough that was wholly typical of him. Then he looked again at the man opposite him, the man charged with wilful murder.

Mr Mayherne was a small man precise in manner, neatly, not to say foppishly dressed, with a pair of very shrewd and piercing grey eyes. By no means a fool. Indeed, as a solicitor, Mr Mayherne's reputation stood very high. His voice, when he spoke to his client, was dry but not unsympathetic.

'I must impress upon you again that you are in very grave danger, and that the utmost frankness is necessary.'

Leonard Vole, who had been staring in a dazed fashion at the blank wall in front of him, transferred his glance to the solicitor.

'I know,' he said hopelessly. 'You keep telling me so. But I can't seem to realize yet that I'm charged with murder – *murder*. And such a dastardly crime too.'

Mr Mayherne was practical, not emotional. He coughed again, took off his pince-nez, polished them carefully, and replaced them on his nose. Then he said:

'Yes, yes, yes. Now, my dear Mr Vole, we're going to make a determined effort to get you off – and we shall succeed – we shall succeed. But I must have all the facts. I must know just how damaging the case against you is likely to be. Then we can fix upon the best line of defence.'

Still the young man looked at him in the same dazed, hopeless fashion. To Mr Mayherne the case had seemed black enough, and the guilt of the prisoner assured. Now, for the first time, he felt a doubt.

'You think I'm guilty,' said Leonard Vole, in a low voice. 'But, by God, I swear I'm not! It looks pretty black against me, I know that. I'm like a man caught in a net – the meshes

witness: s.o who gives his/her testimony in a court of justice
● **prosecution** (noun); prosecute (verb): bring a criminal charge
against s.o in a lawcourt

pince-nez: pair of glasses that clips on the nose ● **cleared his
throat** to have a clear voice ● **dry-as-dust cough:** *raclement de
gorge* ● **wholly:** totally ● **opposite:** facing
charged with: accused of ● **wilful:** intentional ● **murder:**
killing, homicide ● **small** ≠ tall ● **in manner:** in his attitude
● **neatly:** with care ● **foppishly dressed:** wearing refined clothes
(a fop = a dandy) ● **shrewd:** clever ● **by no means:** in no way
● **fool:** stupid person ● **indeed:** certainly ● **solicitor:** lawyer
who advises clients on legal matters ● **stood very high:** was
excellent ● speak, **spoke**, spoken ● **dry:** cold ● **unsympathetic:**
hostile ● **impress upon you:** remind you, make you understand
● **again:** one more time ● **the utmost:** the greatest ● **frankness:**
sincerity, honesty ● **staring:** looking fixedly ● **dazed:** stupefied ●
fashion: manner, way ● **blank:** with no openings ● **glance:** look
hopelessly: desperately ● **keep** + ing: never stop ● **so:** that
(substitute for what precedes) ● **I can't seem ... yet:** up to now
I haven't realized ● **charged with:** accused of ● **dastardly:** vile,
vicious ● **coughed** to clear his throat (cf above)
took off ≠ put on ● **polished** them: cleaned them (note the
plural) ● say, **said**, said

get you off: get you out of trouble ● **we shall succeed**
(determination) ● **I must have** (necessity, obligation)
how damaging ... to be: what risks you are running ● **case:**
lawsuit ● **likely to** (probability) ● **fix upon:** decide about ●
defence (GB) or defen**se** (US) ● **still** (continuation)
hopeless ≠ hopeful; hope ≠ despair
black enough: quite desperate ● **guilt** (noun); be guilty ≠ be
innocent ● feel, **felt**, felt
low ≠ high ● **by God** (excl) ● **swear:** promise, declare solemnly
pretty + adj: quite, very ● **caught** like a fish in a **net** (unable to
escape) ● **meshes:** *mailles*

of it all round me, entangling me whichever way I turn. But I didn't do it, Mr Mayherne, I didn't do it!'

In such a position a man was bound to protest his innocence. Mr Mayherne knew that. Yet, in spite of himself, he was impressed. It might be, after all, that Leonard Vole was innocent.

'You are right, Mr Vole,' he said gravely. 'The case does look very black against you. Nevertheless, I accept your assurance. Now, let us get to facts. I want you to tell me in your own words exactly how you came to make the acquaintance of Miss Emily French.'

'It was one day in Oxford Street. I saw an elderly lady crossing the road. She was carrying a lot of parcels. In the middle of the street she dropped them, tried to recover them, found a bus was almost on top of her and just managed to reach the kerb safely, dazed and bewildered by people having shouted at her. I recovered the parcels, wiped the mud off them as best I could, retied the string of one, and returned them to her.'

'There was no question of your having saved her life?'

'Oh! Dear me, no. All I did was to perform a common act of courtesy. She was extremely grateful, thanked me warmly, and said something about my manners not being those of most of the younger generation – I can't remember the exact words. Then I lifted my hat and went on. I never expected to see her again. But life is full of coincidences. That very evening I came across her at a party at a friend's house. She recognized me at once and asked that I should be introduced to her. I then found out that she was a Miss Emily French and that she lived at Cricklewood. I talked to her for some time. She was, I imagine, an old lady who took sudden violent fancies to people. She took one to me on the strength of a perfectly simple action which anyone might have performed. On leaving, she shook me warmly by the hand, and asked me to come and see her. I replied, of course, that I should be very pleased to do so, and she then urged me to name a day. I did not want particularly to go, but it would have seemed churlish to refuse, so I fixed on the following Saturday. After

entangling me: making me a prisoner ● **whichever:** no matter which

such a position: a situation like this ● **bound:** sure, certain know, **knew**, known ● **yet:** but, nevertheless ● **in spite of himself:** unwillingly ● **it might be** (supposition)

you are right: it is true; be right ≠ be wrong ● <u>**does**</u> look (emphatic) ● **nevertheless:** but, yet, however

assurance: solemn declaration, promise ● **let us** or let's (imperative) ● **in your own words:** yourself ● **make the acquaintance of:** meet, know

elderly: polite word for "old"

crossing: walking across (from one side to the other) ● **parcels:** packets ● **dropped them:** let them fall on the ground ● **recover them:** pick them up ● **found:** realized ● **on top of her:** running over her ● **managed:** succeeded ● **reach:** arrive at ● **curb:** side of the road ● **safely:** unhurt ● **bewildered:** stupefied ● **shouted** <u>**at**</u> (aggressively) ● **wiped ... off them:** cleaned them ● **best** (superlative of "good") ● **retied the str**<u>**ing**</u> around the parcel to make it look presentable ● **your hav**<u>**ing**</u> (gerund) ● **saved her life:** saved her from death ● **dear me:** excl of protest ● **perform:** do ● **common:** simple, ordinary ● **grateful:** thankful, appreciative of the favour ● **warmly:** enthusiastically

most of: the majority of

lifted: raised ● **went on:** continued walking ● **expected to:** thought I would ● **that** <u>**very**</u> **evening** (emphatic): the same evening ● **came across her:** met her by chance ● **party:** occasion when people get together to enjoy themselves ● **at once:** immediately ● **introduced:** presented ● **found out:** discovered ● **a** (certain) Miss Emily French

take, **took**, taken

fancies: fancy (sing): attraction, affection ● **one:** a fancy ● **on the strength of:** because of, on the basis of ● **anyone:** any other person no matter who ● **might** (possibility): could ● **on leaving:** when she left ● **shook me by the hand:** took my hand in hers (to wish me goodbye) ● **come** <u>**and**</u> **see her** ● **replied:** answered ● **should** or would ● **pleased:** glad ● **urged me:** pushed me, encouraged me strongly ● **churlish:** impolite, ill-mannered

she had gone, I learned something about her from my friends. That she was rich, eccentric, lived alone with one maid and owned no less than eight cats.'

'I see,' said Mr Mayherne. 'The question of her being well off came up as early as that?'

'If you mean that I inquired –' began Leonard Vole hotly, but Mr Mayherne stilled him with a gesture.

'I have to look at the case as it will be presented by the other side. An ordinary observer would not have supposed Miss French to be a lady of means. She lived poorly, almost humbly. Unless you had been told the contrary, you would in all probability have considered her to be in poor circumstances – at any rate to begin with. Who was it exactly who told you that she was well off?'

'My friend, George Harvey, at whose house the party took place.'

'Is he likely to remember having done so?'

'I really don't know. Of course it is some time ago now.'

'Quite so, Mr Vole. You see, the first aim of the prosecution will be to establish that you were in low water financially – that is true, is it not?'

Leonard Vole flushed.

'Yes,' he said, in a low voice. 'I'd been having a run of infernal bad luck just then.'

'Quite so,' said Mr Mayherne again. 'That being, as I say, in low water financially, you met this rich old lady and cultivated her acquaintance assiduously. Now if we are in a position to say that you had no idea she was well off, and that you visited her out of pure kindness of heart –'

'Which is the case.'

'I dare say. I am not disputing the point. I am looking at it from the outside point of view. A great deal depends on the memory of Mr Harvey. Is he likely to remember that conversation or is he not? Could he be confused by counsel into believing that it took place later?'

Leonard Vole reflected for some minutes. Then he said steadily enough, but with a rather paler face:

'I do not think that that line would be successful, Mr

learned (or "learnt"): got to know
alone: without any human company ● **maid:** female servant
owned: possessed ● **no less than:** at least, a minimum of
her being (gerund): the fact that she was ● **well-off:** rich,
wealthy ● **came up:** arose, appeared ● **early:** soon
inquired: asked for information ● begin, **began**, begun ● **hotly:**
angrily ● **stilled him:** quietened him, calmed him down

the other side: the opposing party
a lady of means: a rich woman (financial **means**) ● **poorly:**
in a state of poverty ● **unless:** except if ● **you had been told**
(passive): s.o had told you ● **in poor circumstances:** poor,
badly-off ● **at any rate:** in any case
tell, **told**, told
whose house: the house of whom ● **took place:** was held
(hold, held, held)
he is likely to: he will very probably

quite so: exactly ● **aim:** objective, goal
in low water: in a bad situation, in dire straights
true ≠ false
flushed: became red with embarrassment
a run of: a period of
bad luck or bad fortune ≠ good luck, good fortune

acquaintance: social relationship
had no idea: ignored
out of: because of ● **kindness of heart**: consideration,
generosity
I dare say: I am sure ● **disputing**: discussing
a great deal: a lot

counsel: lawyer conducting the case in court (here, for the
opposing party) ● **later** ≠ sooner (cf "as early as that", above)

steadily enough: without too much emotion ● **rather:**
somewhat, slightly ● **line** (of defence)

Mayherne. Several of those present heard his remark, and one or two of them chaffed me about my conquest of a rich old lady.'

The solicitor endeavoured to hide his disappointment with a wave of the hand.

'Unfortunately,' he said. 'But I congratulate you upon your plain speaking, Mr Vole. It is to you I look to guide me. Your judgement is quite right. To persist in the line I spoke of would have been disastrous. We must leave that point. You made the acquaintance of Miss French, you called upon her, the acquaintanceship progressed. We want a clear reason for all this. Why did you, a young man of thirty-three, good-looking, fond of sport, popular with your friends, devote so much time to an elderly woman with whom you could hardly have anything in common?'

Leonard Vole flung out his hands in a nervous gesture.

'I can't tell you – I really can't tell you. After the first visit, she pressed me to come again, spoke of being lonely and unhappy. She made it difficult for me to refuse. She showed so plainly her fondness and affection for me that I was placed in an awkward position. You see, Mr Mayherne, I've got a weak nature – I drift – I'm one of those people who can't say "No." And believe me or not, as you like, after the third or fourth visit I paid her I found myself getting genuinely fond of the old thing. My mother died when I was young, an aunt brought me up, and she too died before I was fifteen. If I told you that I genuinely enjoyed being mothered and pampered, I dare say you'd only laugh.'

Mr Mayherne did not laugh. Instead he took off his pince-nez again and polished them, always a sign with him that he was thinking deeply.

'I accept your explanation, Mr Vole,' he said at last. 'I believe it to be psychologically probable. Whether a jury would take that view of it is another matter. Please continue your narrative. When was it that Miss French first asked you to look into her business affairs?'

'After my third or fourth visit to her. She understood

several: some, a few ● **those:** the people ● hear, **heard**, heard
chaffed me: laughed at me, mocked me, teased me

endeavoured: tried hard ● **hide:** dissimulate (fml)
wave: movement (the waves on the sea)
unfortunately: unluckily (expresses regret) ● **congratulate:**
compliment ● **plain speaking:** sincerity ● **It is to you I look**
(inversion): I count on you ● **I spoke of:** I mentioned

called upon her: visited her, paid her a visit

thirty-three: 33 years-old ● **good-looking**: attractive
fond of: who likes ● **devote**: dedicate
whom: object form of "who" ● **hardly:** only just, scarcely

fling, **flung**, flung **out:** moved quickly
I can't tell you: I don't know
pressed me: insisted upon me, urged me ● **lonely:** unhappy
from being alone ● **unhappy:** sad
plainly: clearly, obviously ● **fondness:** attachment, liking
awkward: difficult
weak: feeble ≠ strong ● **I drift:** I am indecisive, I am easily
influenced ● **third:** 3rd
fourth: 4th ● pay (**paid**, paid) s.o a visit: go and see s.o
● **genuinely:** really, sincerely ● **the old <u>thing</u>** (affectionate term,
here): the old lady ● **aunt:** mother's sister ● bring, **brought**,
brought **me up:** raised me, educated me ● **(being) mothered
and pampered** (passive): treated with care and affection ●
laugh at me: make fun of me, mock me
instead (of): in lieu of
deeply: intensively
explanation (noun); explain (verb) ● **at last:** finally
whether or not
take that view of it: agree with that version of things ● **matter:**
question ● **narrative:** story

understand, **understood**, understood

very little of money matters, and was worried about some investments.'

Mr Mayherne looked up sharply.

'Be careful, Mr Vole. The maid, Janet Mackenzie, declares that her mistress was a good woman of business and transacted all her own affairs, and this is borne out by the testimony of her bankers.'

'I can't help that,' said Vole earnestly. 'That's what she said to me.'

Mr Mayherne looked at him for a moment or two in silence. Though he had no intention of saying so, his belief in Leonard Vole's innocence was at that moment strengthened. He knew something of the mentality of elderly ladies. He saw Miss French, infatuated with the good-looking young man, hunting about for pretexts that should bring him to the house. What more likely than that she should plead ignorance of business, and beg him to help her with her money affairs? She was enough of a woman of the world to realize that any man is slightly flattered by such an admission of his superiority. Leonard Vole had been flattered. Perhaps, too, she had not been averse to letting this young man know that she was wealthy. Emily French had been a strong-willed old woman, willing to pay her price for what she wanted. All this passed rapidly through Mr Mayherne's mind, but he gave no indication of it, and asked instead a further question.

'And you did handle her affairs for her at her request?'

'I did.'

'Mr Vole,' said the solicitor, 'I am going to ask you a very serious question, and one to which it is vital I should have a truthful answer. You were in low water financially. You had the handling of an old lady's affairs – an old lady who, according to her own statement, knew little or nothing of business. Did you at any time, or in any manner, convert to your own use the securities which you handled? Did you engage in any transaction for your own pecuniary advantage which will not bear the light of day?' He quelled the other's response. 'Wait a minute before you answer. There are two courses open to us. Either we can make a feature of your probity and honesty

worried: anxious
investments: sums of money invested in order to make profit
sharply: with a harsh look, severely, sternly
be careful: mind what you say, pay attention to what you say

own: personal ● bear, bore, **borne out:** confirmed
testimony: cf title note
I can't help that: it's not my fault ● **earnestly:** sincerely

though: although ● **belief** (noun); believe (verb) in s.o or sthg
strengthened: made stronger, reinforced
elderly: a polite term for "old"
see, **saw**, seen: imagined ● **infatuated with:** excessively fond of
hunting about for: trying to find, searching for
what more likely than: it is only logical ● **plead ignorance of:**
pretend she didn't know anything about ● **beg him:** ask
him insistently ● **a woman of the world:** a woman who is
experienced in human society ● **admission** (noun); admit (verb):
recognition
averse to: opposed to ● **letting ... know:** informing (him)
wealthy: rich, well-off ● **strong-willed:** very determined
willing to: ready to, prepared to
mind: brain ● give, **gave**, given
a further question: another question, one more question
handle: look after, take care of, deal with ● **request:** demand,
solicitation

truthful: sincere
handling: responsibility
statement: declaration
any: no matter what ● **convert:** transfer ● **your own use:** your
benefit, your advantage ● **securities** (banking term): titles,
certificates of property ● **pecuniary:** financial ● **which will not
bear the light of day:** which is illegal ● **quelled:** stopped
courses (of action): lines of defence
either ... or (alternative) ● **make a feature of:** insist upon

in conducting her affairs whilst pointing out how unlikely it is that you would commit murder to obtain money which you might have obtained by such infinitely easier means. If, on the other hand, there is anything in your dealings which the prosecution will get hold of – if, to put it baldly, it can be proved that you swindled the old lady in any way, we must take the line that you had no motive for the murder, since she was already a profitable source of income to you. You perceive the distinction. Now, I beg of you, take your time before you reply.'

But Leonard Vole took no time at all.

'My dealings with Miss French's affairs are all perfectly fair and above board. I acted for her interests to the very best of my ability, as anyone will find who looks into the matter.'

'Thank you,' said Mr Mayherne. 'You relieve my mind very much. I pay you the compliment of believing that you are far too clever to lie to me over such an important matter.'

'Surely,' said Vole eagerly, 'the strongest point in my favour is the lack of motive. Granted that I cultivated the acquaint-anceship of a rich old lady in the hope of getting money out of her – that, I gather, is the substance of what you have been saying – surely her death frustrates all my hopes?'

The solicitor looked at him steadily. Then, very deliberately, he repeated his unconscious trick with his pince-nez. It was not until they were firmly replaced on his nose that he spoke.

'Are you not aware, Mr Vole, Miss French left a will under which you are the principal beneficiary?'

'What?' The prisoner sprang to his feet. His dismay was obvious and unforced. 'My God! What are you saying? She left her money to me?'

Mr Mayherne nodded slowly. Vole sank down again, his head in his hands.

'You pretend you know nothing of this will?'

'Pretend? There's no pretence about it. I knew nothing about it.'

'What would you say if I told you that the maid, Janet

whilst: while ● **pointing out:** indicating ● **unlikely:** improbable

might (possibility) ● **easier:** simpler ● **means:** ways, manners
on the other hand (introduces an opposite argument) ●
dealings: transactions ● **get hold of:** find ● **to put it baldly:** to
use plain (= direct) language ● **proved:** cf prove (verb); proof
(noun) ● **swindled:** cheated on ● **since:** because, given that
source of income: source of profit
I beg of you: polite for "please"

fair: clear, honest ● **above board:** above suspicion,
irreproachable ● **ability:** capacity ● **looks into the matter:**
examines the case
relieve my mind: free my spirit from worry
pay s.o **a compliment** (note the verb) ● **far** or by far: much
clever: intelligent ● **lie:** tell lies ≠ tell the truth (adj: true ≠ false)
eagerly: with passion ● **the strongest point:** the best argument
lack: absence ● **granted that:** supposing that
in the hope of: with the strong wish or desire to, in the aim of
out of: from ● **I gather:** I suppose, I understand

steadily: impassively, in a calm, controlled way
trick: gesture
not until: not before

Are you not aware: don't you realize ● **leave, left,** left ● **will:**
testament ● **principal:** main
spring, sprang, sprung **to his feet:** stood up suddenly ●
dismay: consternation ● **obvious:** clear, easy to see ● **My
God!:** excl of surprise ● **left:** (here) donated
nodded: moved his head up and down to confirm ● **sank down:**
(here) sat down heavily ● <u>his</u> head in <u>his</u> hands (note the use
of possessive pronouns)

Mackenzie, swears that you *did* know? That her mistress told her distinctly that she had consulted you in the matter, and told you of her intentions?'

'Say? That she's lying! No, I go too fast. Janet is an elderly woman. She was a faithful watchdog to her mistress, and she didn't like me. She was jealous and suspicious. I should say that Miss French confided her intentions to Janet, and that Janet either mistook something she said, or else was convinced in her own mind that I had persuaded the old lady into doing it. I dare say that she believes herself now that Miss French actually told her so.'

'You don't think she dislikes you enough to lie deliberately about the matter?'

Leonard Vole looked shocked and startled.

'No, indeed! Why should she?'

'I don't know,' said Mr Mayherne thoughtfully. 'But she's very bitter against you.'

The wretched young man groaned again.

'I'm beginning to see,' he muttered. 'It's frightful. I made up to her, that's what they'll say, I got her to make a will leaving her money to me, and then I go there that night, and there's nobody in the house – they find her the next day – oh! my God, it's awful!'

'You are wrong about there being nobody in the house,' said Mr Mayherne. 'Janet, as you remember, was to go out for the evening. She went, but about half past nine she returned to fetch the pattern of a blouse sleeve which she had promised to a friend. She let herself in by the back door, went upstairs and fetched it, and went out again. She heard voices in the sitting-room, though she could not distinguish what they said, but she will swear that one of them was Miss French's and one was a man's.'

'At half past nine,' said Leonard Vole. 'At half past nine…' He sprang to his feet. 'But then I'm saved – saved –'

'What do you mean, saved?' cried Mr Mayherne, astonished.

'*By half past nine I was at home again!* My wife can prove that. I left Miss French about five minutes to nine. I arrived

matter: subject, situation, event

lying: telling lies ● **go too fast:** tell things too quickly ● **faithful:** loyal, devoted ● **watchdog:** s.o who defends another person's interests or property
confided: told confidentially
either... or else (alternative) ● mistake, **mistook**, mistaken: misunderstood

actually: really
dislikes: doesn't like ("hates" is stronger)

startled: stupefied

thoughtfully: pensively
bitter: resentful, full of resentment
wretched: poor ● **groaned:** grumbled (sign of complaint, suffering) ● **muttered:** said in a low voice (as if to himself) ●
frightful: terrifying ● **made up to her:** tried to gain her favour ●
got her to: influenced her to
the next day: the following day, the day after
awful: horrible, dreadful
there being (note the use of the gerund): there is/are, there was/were, etc. ● **was** (supposed) **to go out:** "be to" indicates that sthg is planned
fetch: get ● **pattern:** model ● **blouse sleeve:** *manche de chemisier* ● **let herself in:** entered the house ● **back door** ≠ front door ● **upstairs** ≠ downstairs
sitting-room: living-room, lounge
Miss French's voice (elliptical)

saved: out of danger (here: saved from being condemned)

astonished: surprised
half past nine: 9.30 ● **at home again:** back home
five minutes to nine: five minutes before nine, 8.55

home about twenty past nine. My wife was there waiting for me. Oh! Thank God – thank God! And bless Janet Mackenzie's sleeve pattern.'

In his exuberance, he hardly noticed that the grave expression of the solicitor's face had not altered. But the latter's words brought him down to earth with a bump.

'Who, then, in your opinion, murdered Miss French?'

'Why, a burglar, of course, as was thought at first. The window was forced, you remember. She was killed with a heavy blow from a crowbar, and the crowbar was found lying on the floor beside the body. And several articles were missing. But for Janet's absurd suspicions and dislike of me, the police would never have swerved from the right track.'

'That will hardly do, Mr Vole,' said the solicitor. 'The things that were missing were mere trifles of no value, taken as a blind. And the marks on the window were not all conclusive. Besides, think for yourself. You say you were no longer in the house by half past nine. Who, then, was the man Janet heard talking to Miss French in the sitting-room? She would hardly be having an amicable conversation with a burglar?'

'No,' said Vole. 'No –' He looked puzzled and discouraged. 'But anyway,' he added with reviving spirit, 'it lets me out. I've got an alibi. You must see Romaine – my wife – at once.'

'Certainly,' acquiesced the lawyer. 'I should already have seen Mrs Vole but for her being absent when you were arrested. I wired to Scotland at once, and I understand that she arrives back tonight. I am going to call upon her immediately I leave here.'

Vole nodded, a great expression of satisfaction settling down over his face.

'Yes, Romaine will tell you. My God! it's a lucky chance that.'

'Excuse me, Mr Vole, but you are very fond of your wife?'

'Of course.'

'And she of you?'

twenty past nine: 9.20
Thank God!: excl of relief ● **bless:** excl of satisfaction, of thankfulness
hardly noticed: didn't see
altered: changed ● **the latter** (refers to the person just mentioned) ● **brought him ... bump:** made him come back to reality abruptly ● **murdered:** killed
why: (here) well ● **a burglar** enters a house illegally to steal

heavy blow: hard stroke ● **crowbar:** iron bar used as a lever
lying (cf verb lie, lay, lain) ● **beside:** near ● (dead) **body** or corpse ● **(were) missing:** had disappeared ● **but for:** without
swerved: changed direction ● **the right track:** the good direction (for the investigation) ● **that will hardly do:** your explanation is not convincing ● **mere trifles:** unimportant things ● **taken:** stolen (steal, stole, stolen) ● **a blind:** a cover (to lead the investigation on the wrong track) ● **conclusive:** decisive ● **besides:** moreover ● **no longer:** not any more

hardly (adv indicating improbability) ● **amicable:** friendly
puzzled: perplexed, confused
added: said in addition ● **reviving spirit:** regained optimism
it lets me out: it exonerates me ● **wife:** man's partner in marriage
acquiesced: agreed
but for her being absent: if she had not been absent
wired: sent a telegram ● **Scotland**, England and Wales = G.B
arrives back: returns ● **tonight:** this evening ● **immediately:** as soon as
settling down: becoming visible

a lucky chance: a wonderful opportunity

of course: certainly, undoubtedly

'Romaine is devoted to me. She'd do anything in the world for me.'

He spoke enthusiastically, but the solicitor's heart sank a little lower. The testimony of a devoted wife – would it gain credence?

'Was there anyone else who saw you return at nine-twenty? A maid, for instance?'

'We have no maid.'

'Did you meet anyone in the street on the way back?'

'Nobody I knew. I rode part of the way in a bus. The conductor might remember.'

Mr Mayherne shook his head doubtfully.

'There is no one, then, who can confirm your wife's testimony?'

'No. But it isn't necessary, surely?'

'I dare say not. I dare say not,' said Mr Mayherne hastily. 'Now there's just one thing more. Did Miss French know that you were a married man?'

'Oh, yes.'

'Yet you never took your wife to see her. Why was that?'

For the first time, Leonard Vole's answer came halting and uncertain.

'Well – I don't know.'

'Are you aware that Janet Mackenzie says her mistress believed you to be single, and contemplated marrying you in the future?'

Vole laughed.

'Absurd! There was forty years difference in age between us.'

'It has been done,' said the solicitor drily. 'The fact remains. Your wife never met Miss French?'

'No –' Again the constraint.

'You will permit me to say,' said the lawyer, 'that I hardly understand your attitude in the matter.'

Vole flushed, hesitated, and then spoke.

'I'll make a clean breast of it. I was hard up, as you know. I hoped that Miss French might lend me some money. She was fond of me, but she wasn't at all interested in the strug-

devoted: loyal ● **anything in the world:** anything she could

(his) heart sank (sink, sank, sunk): a feeling of discouragement
invaded him (**heart:** centre of emotions)
gain credence: be considered as valid
anyone else: another person ● **nine-twenty** or twenty past nine:
9.20 ● **for instance:** for example

ride, **rode**, ridden (a horse, a bicycle, a train, a taxi, a bus ...)
conductor: s.o who collects fares from passengers or checks
their tickets ● **shook his head:** moved his head from left to right
(shake, shook, shaken)

I dare say not: I don't think so, I think it isn't ● **hastily:** very
quickly, hurriedly
a married man ≠ a single man, a bachelor

yet (contradiction): nevertheless ● **took:** went with
halting: unsure, hesitant

single: unmarried ● **contemplated** + ing: thought about + ing,
planned to
laughed to express his disbelief

It has been done: it has already happened ● **drily:** in a dry or
harsh tone ● **remains:** (here) is there
constraint: embarrassment
I hardly understand: I don't quite understand

flushed: became red in the face
make a clean breast of it: make a confession ● **hard up** (fam):
in need of money, poor ● **lend**, lent, lent (money): provide money
temporarily upon promise of return ● **was fond of me:** liked me

gles of a young couple. Early on, I found that she had taken it for granted that my wife and I didn't get on – were living apart. Mr Mayherne – I wanted the money – for Romaine's sake. I said nothing, and allowed the old lady to think what she chose. She spoke of my being an adopted son for her. There was never any question of marriage – that must be just Janet's imagination.'

'And that is all?'

'Yes – that is all.'

Was there just a shade of hesitation in the words? The lawyer fancied so. He rose and held out his hand.

'Goodbye, Mr Vole.' He looked into the haggard young face and spoke with an unusual impulse. 'I believe in your innocence in spite of the multitude of facts arrayed against you. I hope to prove it and vindicate you completely.'

Vole smiled back at him.

'You'll find the alibi is all right,' he said cheerfully.

Again he hardly noticed that the other did not respond.

'The whole thing hinges a good deal on the testimony of Janet Mackenzie,' said Mr Mayherne. 'She hates you. That much is clear.'

'She can hardly hate me,' protested the young man.

The solicitor shook his head as he went out.

'Now for Mrs Vole,' he said to himself.

He was seriously disturbed by the way the thing was shaping.

The Voles lived in a small shabby house near Paddington Green. It was to this house that Mr Mayherne went.

In answer to his ring, a big slatternly woman, obviously a charwoman, answered the door.

'Mrs Vole? Has she returned yet?'

'Got back an hour ago. But I dunno if you can see her.'

'If you will take my card to her,' said Mr Mayherne quietly, 'I am quite sure that she will do so.'

The woman looked at him doubtfully, wiped her hand on her apron and took the card. Then she closed the door in his face and left him on the step outside.

(life's) **struggles** or difficulties ● **early on:** right from the beginning ● **taken it for granted:** been convinced ● **didn't get on:** didn't live in perfect harmony ● **apart:** separately
sake: own benefit
choose, **chose**, chosen: wanted ● **son:** male child; daughter: female child

all: everything, the whole story
shade: touch
fancied so: thought there was ● rise, **rose**, risen (from his seat): stood up
unusual: uncommon ● (with an) **impulse:** instinctively
in spite of: regardless of ● **arrayed:** gathered, collected
vindicate you: prove you are innocent (not guilty)

cheerfully: happily

hinges on: depends on ● **a good deal:** very much, a lot
hates you: dislikes you greatly (love ≠ hate or hatred)

disturbed: perturbed ● **the way the thing was shaping:** the evolution of the situation

shabby: dilapidated, dirty and untidy

(doorbell) **ring** ● **slatternly:** dirty and untidy ● **obviously:** visibly
charwoman: woman whose job consists in cleaning the house

(she) **got back** (elliptical) ● **dunno** (conversational language): don't know ● **will:** would like to (polite request) ● **quietly:** calmly
do so: accept to see me
wiped: rubbed (her hand) to clean it
apron: protection for clothes when doing the housework (worn over the front part of the body) ● door(**step**) or threshold

In a few minutes, however, she returned with a slightly altered manner.

'Come inside, please.'

She ushered him into a tiny drawing-room. Mr Mayherne, examining a drawing on the wall, stared up suddenly to face a tall pale woman who had entered so quietly that he had not heard her.

'Mr Mayherne? You are my husband's solicitor, are you not? You have come from him? Will you please sit down?'

Until she spoke he had not realized that she was not English. Now, observing her more closely, he noticed the high cheekbones, the dense blue-black of the hair, and an occasional very slight movement of the hands that was distinctly foreign. A strange woman, very quiet. So quiet as to make one uneasy. From the very first Mr Mayherne was conscious that he was up against something that he did not understand.

'Now, my dear Mrs Vole,' he began, 'you must not give way –'

He stopped. It was so very obvious that Romaine Vole had not the slightest intention of giving way. She was perfectly calm and composed.

'Will you please tell me all about it?' she said. 'I must know everything. Do not think to spare me. I want to know the worst.' She hesitated, then repeated in a lower tone, with a curious emphasis which the lawyer did not understand: 'I want to know the worst.'

Mr Mayherne went over his interview with Leonard Vole. She listened attentively, nodding her head now and then.

'I see,' she said, when he had finished. 'He wants me to say that he came in at twenty minutes past nine that night?'

'He did come in at that time?' said Mr Mayherne sharply.

'That is not the point,' she said coldly. 'Will my saying so acquit him? Will they believe me?'

Mr Mayherne was taken aback. She had gone so quickly to the core of the matter.

altered manner: different attitude

ushered him: led him (lead, led, led) ● **tiny:** very small ●
drawing-room: sitting-room ● **drawing:** picture drawn but not
coloured ● **stared:** looked fixedly ● **tall** ≠ small

husband: woman's partner in marriage
come from him: been sent by him, on his behalf

more closely: with more attention, more carefully
cheekbones: prominent bones on each side of the face below
the eyes ● **slight:** small, almost imperceptible
foreign: characteristic of another country
one (impersonal): anybody ● **uneasy:** ill-at-ease ● **the very
first:** the beginning ● **he was up against:** he had to deal with (to
cope with, to face)
give way: give up, renounce

the slightest (superlative) cf slight, above
composed: calm, self-controlled, serene

... to spare me: don't hesitate to tell me the truth
the worst ≠ the best ● **lower** ≠ louder (sound)
emphasis: insistence

went over: related, recounted
now and then: from time to time

he did come in (emphatic)
sharply: in a harsh tone, not very nicely
the point: the question ● **my saying so** (gerund): the fact that I
say that
taken aback: disconcerted, startled, shocked
the core: the heart, the centre

'That is what I want to know,' she said. 'Will it be enough? Is there anyone else who can support my evidence?'

There was a suppressed eagerness in her manner that made him vaguely uneasy.

'So far there is no one else,' he said reluctantly.

'I see,' said Romaine Vole.

She sat for a minute or two perfectly still. A little smile played over her lips.

The lawyer's feeling of alarm grew stronger and stronger.

'Mrs Vole –' he began. 'I know what you must feel –'

'Do you?' she said. 'I wonder.'

'In the circumstances –'

'In the circumstances – I intend to play a lone hand.'

He looked at her in dismay.

'But, my dear Mrs Vole – you are overwrought. Being so devoted to your husband –'

'I beg your pardon?'

The sharpness of her voice made him start. He repeated in a hesitating manner:

'Being so devoted to your husband –'

Romaine Vole nodded slowly, the same strange smile on her lips.

'Did he tell you that I was devoted to him?' she asked softly. 'Ah! yes, I can see he did. How stupid men are! Stupid – stupid – stupid –'

She rose suddenly to her feet. All the intense emotion that the lawyer had been conscious of in the atmosphere was now concentrated in her tone.

'I hate him, I tell you! I hate him. I hate him, I hate him! I would like to see him hanged by the neck till he is dead.'

The lawyer recoiled before her and the smouldering passion in her eyes.

She advanced a step nearer, and continued vehemently:

'Perhaps I *shall* see it. Supposing I tell you that he did not come in that night at twenty past nine, but at twenty past *ten?* You say that he tells you he knew nothing about the money coming to him. Supposing I tell you he knew all

enough: sufficient
support or give support to ● **evidence:** (here) testimony
suppressed: controlled ● **eagerness:** impatient desire

so far: up to now, until the present time ● **reluctantly:** unwillingly

sit, sat, sat ● **still:** immobile ● **smile:** expression of satisfaction
lips: upper lip and lower lip (mouth)
feeling of alarm: sensation of worry ● **grew stronger and**
stronger: became more and more important; grow, grew, grown

I wonder: I have doubts

intend to: have planned to ● **play a lone hand:** testify (in court)
without any assistance ● **dismay:** consternation
overwrought: too nervous and emotional

I beg your pardon? (formal): "pardon?" is more commonly used
sharpness: abruptness ● **start:** jump

softly: gently ● **how** + adj or adv (exclamation)

rise, rose, risen **to her feet** (sing foot): stood up

hate: loathe ≠ love
hanged: executed by being suspended from a rope tied round
the **neck** ● **till:** until ● **recoiled:** hesitated ● **smouldering:**
restrained (but very present!)
a step nearer: a short distance closer to him

about it, and counted on it, and committed murder to get it? Supposing I tell you that he admitted to me that night when he came in what he had done? That there was blood on his coat? What then? Supposing that I stand up in court and say all these things?'

Her eyes seemed to challenge him. With an effort, he concealed his growing dismay, and endeavoured to speak in a rational tone.

'You cannot be asked to give evidence against your own husband –'

'He is not my husband!'

The words came out so quickly that he fancied he had misunderstood her.

'I beg your pardon? I –'

'He is not my husband.'

The silence was so intense that you could have heard a pin drop.

'I was an actress in Vienna. My husband is alive but in a madhouse. So we could not marry. I am glad now.'

She nodded defiantly.

'I should like you to tell me one thing,' said Mr Mayherne. He contrived to appear as cool and unemotional as ever. 'Why are you so bitter against Leonard Vole?'

She shook her head, smiling a little.

'Yes, you would like to know. But I shall not tell you. I will keep my secret…'

Mr Mayherne gave his dry little cough and rose.

'There seems no point in prolonging this interview,' he remarked. 'You will hear from me again after I have communicated with my client.'

She came closer to him, looking into his eyes with her own wonderful dark ones.

'Tell me,' she said, 'did you believe – honestly – that he was innocent when you came here today?'

'I did,' said Mr Mayherne.

'You poor little man,' she laughed.

'And I believe so still,' finished the lawyer. 'Good evening, madam.'

blood: red liquid that flows in the veins
coat: outdoor article of clothing

challenge: defy
concealed: hid (hide, hid, hidden)

give evidence: testify

fancied: believed
misunderstood: understood wrongly

... a pin drop: note that the image is different in English and in French! ● **alive** ≠ dead
madhouse (fam): mental hospital or lunatic asylum ● **glad:** happy
defiantly: in a provocative or challenging manner

contrived: managed ● **appear:** look ● **as** (+ adj) **as ever:** as (+ adj) as possible

dry cough: cf 2nd line of the story
there seems no point in + ing: I don't see any interest in + ing
hear from: get news from

closer: nearer
wonderful: extremely beautiful

I believe so still: I continue to think so (= that he is innocent)
madam: polite way of addressing a lady; "Sir", for a man

He went out of the room, taking with him the memory of her startled face.

'This is going to be the devil of a business,' said Mr Mayherne to himself as he strode along the street.

Extraordinary, the whole thing. An extraordinary woman. A very dangerous woman. Women were the devil when they got their knife into you.

What was to be done? That wretched young man hadn't a leg to stand upon. Of course, possibly he did commit the crime...

'No,' said Mr Mayherne to himself. 'No – there's almost too much evidence against him. I don't believe this woman. She was trumping up the whole story. But she'll never bring it into court.'

He wished he felt more conviction on the point.

The police court proceedings were brief and dramatic. The principal witnesses for the prosecution were Janet Mackenzie, maid to the dead woman, and Romaine Heilger, Austrian subject, the mistress of the prisoner.

Mr Mayherne sat in the court and listened to the damning story that the latter told. It was on the lines she had indicated to him in their interview.

The prisoner reserved his defence and was committed for trial.

Mr Mayherne was at his wits' end. The case against Leonard Vole was black beyond words. Even the famous KC who was engaged for the defence held out little hope.

'If we can shake that Austrian woman's testimony, we might do something,' he said dubiously. 'But it's a bad business.'

Mr Mayherne had concentrated his energies on one single point. Assuming Leonard Vole to be speaking the truth, and to have left the murdered woman's house at nine o'clock, who was the man whom Janet heard talking to Miss French at half past nine?

The only ray of light was in the shape of a scapegrace nephew who had in bygone days cajoled and threatened his aunt out of various sums of money. Janet Mackenzie, the

memory (noun); **remember** (verb)

the devil of a ... (fam, intensifier: the hell of a ...): a very difficult ... • **stride, strode, stridden**: walked with long regular steps
whole: entire
the devil: (here) very cruel; cf the Devil or Satan
got their knife into you: considered you and treated you as
their enemy • **wretched**: poor
a leg to stand upon (image): any basis for his defence, any
argument in his favour

too much evidence: too many proofs
trumping up: inventing, making up

wished: would have liked to; wish + preterite (expression of a
regret)
proceedings: legal action or debates • **dramatic**: spectacular,
theatrical
Austrian: from Austria, a republic in central Europe whose
capital is Vienna • **subject**: citizen • **mistress**: illicit lover
damning: proving s.o guilty, likely to lead to s.o's condemnation

interview: discussion
committed for trial: sent to prison until the **trial** (examination of
his case by a judge in a lawcourt) took place
at his wits'end: so worried that he didn't know what to do
black beyond words: absolutely hopeless • **KC** or King's
Counsel: barrister appointed Counsel to the Crown (high rank)
• **held out little hope**: was very pessimistic • **shake**: counter-
act • **testimony** (cf title note) • **dubiously**: doubtfully • **a bad
business**: a difficult case • **one single point**: one point only •
assuming: supposing • **speaking** (or telling) **the truth** ≠ telling
lies; true ≠ false

ray of light: (here) touch of hope • **shape**: form • **scapegrace**:
good-for-nothing • **nephew** (masc); niece (fem) • **bygone**: past
• **threatened**: menaced • **out of**: so as to obtain

solicitor learned, had always been attached to this young man, and had never ceased urging his claims upon her mistress. It certainly seemed possible that it was this nephew who had been with Miss French after Leonard Vole left, especially as he was not to be found in any of his old haunts.

In all other directions, the lawyer's researches had been negative in their result. No one had seen Leonard Vole entering his own house, or leaving that of Miss French. No one had seen any other man enter or leave the house in Cricklewood. All inquiries drew blank.

It was the eve of the trial when Mr Mayherne received the letter which was to lead his thoughts in an entirely new direction.

It came by the six o'clock post. An illiterate scrawl, written on common paper and enclosed in a dirty envelope with the stamp stuck on crooked.

Mr Mayherne read it through once or twice before he grasped its meaning.

Dear Mister:
Youre the lawyer chap wot acks for the young feller, if you want that painted foreign hussy showd up for wot she is an her pack of lies you come to 16 Shaw's Rents Stepney tonight. It ul cawst you 2 hundred quid Arsk for Missis Mogson.

The solicitor read and re-read this strange epistle. It might, of course, be a hoax, but when he thought it over, he became increasingly convinced that it was genuine, and also convinced that it was the one hope for the prisoner. The evidence of Romaine Heilger damned him completely, and the line the defence meant to pursue, the line that the evidence of a woman who had admittedly lived an immoral life was not to be trusted, was at best a weak one.

Mr Mayherne's mind was made up. It was his duty to save his client at all costs. He must go to Shaw's Rents.

He had some difficulty in finding the place, a ramshackle building in an evil-smelling slum, but at last he did so, and

urging his claims: encouraging him in his demands

he was not to be found: it was impossible to find him ● **his old haunts:** the places he frequently visited

entering his house (no preposition!)

inquiries or enquiries: researches ● **drew blank:** were unsuccessful ● **eve:** evening or day before; New Year's Eve ● **trial:** prosecution ● **lead his thoughts:** make him think; think (verb); a thought (noun)
scrawl: bad writing ● write, wrote, **written**
common: ordinary ● **dirty:** not clean
stick, stuck, **stuck** ● (postage) **stamp** ● **crooked:** not straight
through: from A to Z ● **once or twice:** one or two times
grasped its meaning: understood what it meant (cf mean, meant, meant)
Dear Mister: instead of Dear Sir (Mister should precede a family name) ● **youre:** you're ● **chap** (fam): man ● **wot:** who ● **acks:** acts ● **feller:** fellow (fam): man ● **painted** with make-up ● **hussy:** indecent woman ● **showd up:** discovered ● **an:** and ● **pack of lies:** tissue of lies ● **ul:** will ● **cawst:** cost ● **2 hundred quid** (fam): £200 = 200 pounds ● **Missis** or Mrs

epistle (fml): letter
hoax: trick, joke ● **thought it over:** considered it carefully
increasingly: more and more ● **convinced:** certain ● **genuine:** real, authentic ● **the one:** the only
damned: condemned
meant to pursue: intended to follow
was not to be trusted: could not be regarded as valid
at best a weak one: not guaranteed to be successful at all
(his) mind was made up: he had decided ● **duty:** moral obligation ● **at all costs:** at any price
ramshackle: falling to pieces, needing repair, rickety ● **evil-smelling:** foul-smelling, nauseating ● **slum:** poor section of a city

on inquiry for Mrs Mogson was sent up to a room on the third floor. On this door he knocked and getting no answer, knocked again.

At this second knock, he heard a shuffling sound inside, and presently the door was opened cautiously half an inch and a bent figure peered out.

Suddenly the woman, for it was a woman, gave a chuckle and opened the door wider.

'So it's you, dearie,' she said, in a wheezy voice. 'Nobody with you, is there? No playing tricks? That's right. You can come in – you can come in.'

With some reluctance the lawyer stepped across the threshold into the small dirty room, with its flickering gas jet. There was an untidy unmade bed in a corner, a plain deal table and two rickety chairs. For the first time Mr Mayherne had a full view of the tenant of this unsavoury apartment. She was a woman of middle age, bent in figure, with a mass of untidy grey hair and a scarf wound tightly round her face. She saw him looking at this and laughed again, the same curious toneless chuckle.

'Wondering why I hide my beauty, dear? He, he, he. Afraid it may tempt you, eh? But you shall see – you shall see.'

She drew aside the scarf and the lawyer recoiled involuntarily before the almost formless blur of scarlet. She replaced the scarf again.

'So you're not wanting to kiss me, dearie? He, he, I don't wonder. And yet I was a pretty girl once – not so long ago as you'd think, either. Vitriol, dearie, vitriol – that's what did that. Ah! but I'll be even with em –'

She burst into a hideous torrent of profanity which Mr Mayherne tried vainly to quell. She fell silent at last, her hands clenching and unclenching themselves nervously.

'Enough of that,' said the lawyer sternly. 'I've come here because I have reason to believe you can give me information which will clear my client, Leonard Vole. Is that the case?'

Her eye leered at him cunningly.

'What about the money, dearie?' she wheezed. 'Two hundred quid, you remember.'

on inquiry: when he asked ● send, sent, **sent up:** directed upstairs ● ground floor, first floor, second floor, **third floor**, etc. ● you **knock** on the door before entering s.o's house
shuffling sound: noise made by feet moving slowly
cautiously: with care ● **presently:** before long ● **an inch:** 2,54 cm ● **bent:** inclined ● **figure:** form ● **peered out:** looked outside intently ● **for:** because ● **chuckle:** half-suppressed laugh
wid<u>er</u>: comparative form of "wide"; wide-open: fully open
dearie (sarcastic): dear ● **wheezy:** whistling (sign of breathing difficulty) ● **playing tricks:** cheating; trick: malicious action

reluctance: hesitation ● **stepped:** walked
threshold: entrance ● **flickering:** not steady ● **gas jet:** burner on gas cooker ● **untidy:** messy ● **unmade** (verb: <u>make</u> a bed) ●
plain: simple ● **deal table:** table used to play cards on ● **rickety:** needing repair ● **tenant:** occupant ● **unsavoury:** unpleasant ● **apartment** or flat ● **of middle age:** around 40-50 years old ● bend, **bent**, bent ● **scarf:** triangular piece of cloth ● **wound tightly:** *noué serré*
toneless: without tone, inexpressive
(you are) **wondering:** asking yourself ● **I hide:** I don't want to show ● **may** (possibility)
drew aside: took off ● **recoiled:** moved back because of fear or disgust ● **formless:** irregular ● **blur:** mark ● **scarlet:** bright red

kiss: you can kiss s.o on the cheek (friendly kiss) or on the lips (love kiss) ● **I don't wonder:** I am not surprised ● **pretty:** good-looking ● **once:** before
be even with: have my revenge upon ● **em** for "them"
burst into: suddenly started to utter ● **profanity:** obscenity
vainly: in vain ● **quell:** stop ● fall, **fell**, fallen **silent:** stopped speaking ● **clenching and unclenching:** opening and closing in a nervous gesture ● **enough of that:** that's enough, stop it now ● **sternly:** firmly ● **informatio<u>n</u>** (sing)
clear: exonerate
leered at him: looked at him maliciously ● **cunningly:** treacherously ● **wheezed** (breathing with difficulty)

'It is your duty to give evidence, and you can be called upon to do so.'

'That won't do, dearie. I'm an old woman, and I know nothing. But you give me two hundred quid, and perhaps I can give you a hint or two. See?'

'What kind of hint?'

'What should you say to a letter? A letter from *her*. Never mind now how I got hold of it. That's my business. It'll do the trick. But I want my two hundred quid.'

Mr Mayherne looked at her coldly, and made up his mind.

'I'll give you ten pounds, nothing more. And only that if this letter is what you say it is.'

'Ten pounds?' She screamed and raved at him.

'Twenty,' said Mr Mayherne, 'and that's my last word.'

He rose as if to go. Then, watching her closely, he drew out a pocket book, and counted out twenty one-pound notes.

'You see,' he said. 'That is all I have with me. You can take it or leave it.'

But already he knew that the sight of the money was too much for her. She cursed and raved impotently, but at last she gave in. Going over to the bed, she drew something out from beneath the tattered mattress.

'Here you are, damn you!' she snarled. 'It's the top one you want.'

It was a bundle of letters that she threw to him, and Mr Mayherne untied them and scanned them in his usual cool, methodical manner. The woman, watching him eagerly, could gain no clue from his impassive face.

He read each letter through, then returned again to the top one and read it a second time. Then he tied the whole bundle up again carefully.

They were love letters, written by Romaine Heilger, and the man they were written to was not Leonard Vole. The top letter was dated the day of the latter's arrest.

'I spoke true, dearie, didn't I?' whined the woman. 'It'll do for her, that letter?'

be called upon: be asked (passive)

that won't do: that's unnecessary, that's useless

hint: small indication, suggestion, clue
kind: sort
what should you say to...?: what about? ● **never mind:** it doesn't matter
do the trick: be good enough
made up his mind: decided

screamed: shouted very loudly ● **raved at him:** was furious against him ● **last:** final
as if to go: pretending he was leaving ● **drew out:** took out
pocket book: wallet (for money and personal papers) ●
bank**notes:** money comes in the form of notes (paper) or coins (metal) ● **"take it or leave it"** (common phrase): that's my last offer ● **sight:** view, vision
cursed: said obscene words ● **impotently:** feeling powerless
gave in: abandoned, (here) accepted the deal
beneath: under ● **tattered:** old and dirty ● **mattress:** top part of the bed ● **snarled:** said angrily ● **the top one:** the first one at the top (≠ the bottom) ● **want:** (here) need
bundle: pile (of letters) tied together ● throw, **threw**, thrown
untied them: undid the string around the bundle ● **scanned:** examined ● **eagerly:** impatiently
gain no clue: guess nothing
through: completely, from beginning to end, from A to Z
tied (up): fastened the string around the bundle (cf untied, above)

spoke true (incorrect, familiar language): told the truth ● **whined:** said plaintively

Mr Mayherne put the letters in his pocket, then he asked a question.

'How did you get hold of this correspondence?'

'That's telling,' she said with a leer. 'But I know something more. I heard in court what that hussy said. Find out where *she* was at twenty past ten, the time she says she was at home. Ask at the Lion Road Cinema. They'll remember – a fine upstanding girl like that – curse her!'

'Who is the man?' asked Mr Mayherne. 'There's only a Christian name here.'

The other's voice grew thick and hoarse, her hands clenched and unclenched. Finally she lifted one to her face.

'He's the man that did this to me. Many years ago now. She took him away from me – a chit of a girl she was then. And when I went after him – and went for him too – he threw the cursed stuff at me! And she laughed – damn her! I've had it in for her for years. Followed her, I have, spied upon her. And now I've got her! She'll suffer for this, won't she, Mr Lawyer? She'll suffer?'

'She will probably be sentenced to a term of imprisonment for perjury,' said Mr Mayherne quietly.

'Shut away – that's what I want. You're going, are you? Where's my money? Where's that good money?'

Without a word, Mr Mayherne put down the notes on the table. Then, drawing a deep breath, he turned and left the squalid room. Looking back, he saw the old woman crooning over the money.

He wasted no time. He found the cinema in Lion Road easily enough, and, shown a photograph of Romaine Heilger, the commissionaire recognized her at once. She had arrived at the cinema with a man some time after ten o'clock on the evening in question. He had not noticed her escort particularly, but he remembered the lady who had spoken to him about the picture that was showing. They stayed until the end, about an hour later.

Mr Mayherne was satisfied. Romaine Heilger's evidence was a tissue of lies from beginning to end. She had evolved it out of her passionate hatred. The lawyer wondered whether

get hold of: get, acquire, obtain, find
that's telling: those letters say a lot ● **leer:** malicious look

fine: lovely ● **upstanding:** strong and healthy ● **curse her!:** damn her!
Christian name: first name ≠ family name, last name, surname
thick: not clear (because of emotion) ● **hoarse:** sounding harsh, raucous ● **lifted:** raised

took him away: turned him away, stole him! ● **a chit of a girl:** an impudent self-confident young girl
stuff (imprecise): thing
I've had it in for her: I have wanted to get my revenge upon her ● **spied:** cf verb spy: search information secretly; a spy (plur spies) ● **Mr Lawyer:** note the way she calls Mr Mayherne by referring to his job ● **sentenced:** condemned ● **term:** period
perjury: (legal term) lying, hiding the truth voluntarily
shut away: locked up (in a prison cell)

without a word: silently
drawing a deep breath: breathing in air (inhaling) intensely
squalid: dirty and unpleasant ● **crooning:** singing to herself softly
wasted no time: hurried; waste time or money: use up unnecessarily ● **easily enough:** without too much difficulty ● show, showed, **shown** ● **commissionnaire:** uniformed doorman at a cinema, hotel, etc.
escort: person who accompanies another for entertainment

picture: film ● **was showing:** was <u>on</u> (at the cinema)

a tissue of lies: a pack of lies ● **evolved:** invented
out of: because of ● **hatred:** hate ≠ love ● **whether:** if

he would ever know what lay behind that hatred. What had Leonard Vole done to her? He had seemed dumbfounded when the solicitor had reported her attitude to him. He had declared earnestly that such a thing was incredible – yet it had seemed to Mr Mayherne that after the first astonishment his protests had lacked sincerity.

He *did* know. Mr Mayherne was convinced of it. He knew, but had no intention of revealing the fact. The secret between those two remained a secret. Mr Mayherne wondered if some day he should come to learn what it was.

The solicitor glanced at his watch. It was late, but time was everything. He hailed a taxi and gave an address.

'Sir Charles must know of this at once,' he murmured to himself as he got in. The trial of Leonard Vole for the murder of Emily French aroused widespread interest. In the first place the prisoner was young and good-looking, then he was accused of a particularly dastardly crime, and there was the further interest of Romaine Heilger, the principal witness for the prosecution. There had been pictures of her in many papers, and several fictitious stories as to her origin and history.

The proceedings opened quietly enough. Various technical evidence came first. Then Janet Mackenzie was called. She told substantially the same story as before. In cross-examination counsel for the defence succeeded in getting her to contradict herself once or twice over her account of Vole's association with Miss French, he emphasized the fact that though she had heard a man's voice in the sitting-room that night, there was nothing to show that it was Vole who was there, and he managed to drive home a feeling that jealousy and dislike of the prisoner were at the bottom of a good deal of her evidence.

Then the next witness was called.

'Your name is Romaine Heilger?'

'Yes.'

'You are an Austrian subject?'

'Yes.'

lay behind: was at the origin of, had caused
dumbfounded: so stupefied that he was dumb (= unable to speak)
earnestly: sincerely ● **incredible:** unbelievable
astonishment: surprise
had lacked sincerity: had not been sincere

glanced (= gave a quick look) at his watch to see what time it was ● **hailed:** called attention with a signal of the hand ● **address** (double d)
got in (the taxi); get in ≠ get off
aroused: caused, created ● **widespread:** great, important
in the first place: first of all, firstly ● **then:** in addition
dastardly: bad, wicked, brutal

pictures: photographs
papers: or newspapers ● **fictitious**: invented ≠ real, true
history: past, background

cross-examination: second questioning of a witness in order to test the answers given the first time ● **succeeded:** was successful ● **account:** description, report
emphasized: insisted upon

show: prove
drive home (to the court): make the court understand ● **feeling:** impression ● **dislike:** aversion, antipathy ● **at the bottom:** at the origin ● **a good deal of:** the major part of

'For the last three years you have lived with the prisoner and passed yourself off as his wife?'

Just for a moment Romaine Heilger's eye met those of the man in the dock. Her expression held something curious and unfathomable.

'Yes.'

The questions went on. Word by word the damning facts came out. On the night in question the prisoner had taken out a crowbar with him. He had returned at twenty minutes past ten, and had confessed to having killed the old lady. His cuffs had been stained with blood, and he had burned them in the kitchen stove. He had terrorized her into silence by means of threats.

As the story proceeded, the feeling of the court which had, to begin with, been slightly favourable to the prisoner, now set dead against him. He himself sat with downcast head and moody air, as though he knew he were doomed.

Yet it might have been noted that her own counsel sought to restrain Romaine's animosity. He would have preferred her to be a more unbiased witness.

Formidable and ponderous, counsel for the defence arose.

He put it to her that her story was a malicious fabrication from start to finish, that she had not even been in her own house at the time in question, that she was in love with another man and was deliberately seeking to send Vole to his death for a crime he did not commit.

Romaine denied these allegations with superb insolence.

Then came the surprising denouement, the production of the letter. It was read aloud in court in the midst of a breathless stillness.

Max, beloved, the Fates have delivered him into our hands! He has been arrested for murder – but, yes, the murder of an old lady! Leonard who would not hurt a fly! At last I shall have my revenge. The poor chicken! I shall say that he came in that night with blood upon him – that he confessed to me. I shall hang him, Max

passed yourself off: pretended to be

dock: enclosed space where the accused sits or stands during the trial • **unfathomable:** strange, mysterious

went on: continued

cuffs: *manchettes (de chemise)* • **stained:** marked • **burned** with fire • **stove:** (here) gas stove, gas cooker
by means of threats: by menacing her
proceeded: evolved
slightly: rather, somewhat
set dead against: became hostile to • **with downcast head:** looking downward (sign of discouragement) • **moody:** sad • **doomed:** inevitably lost • seek, sought, **sought:** tried

unbiased: impartial, fair
formidable: inspiring fear and respect • **ponderous:** solemn
arise, **arose**, arisen: stood up
put it to her: told her • **fabrication:** invention
from start to finish: from beginning to end

seeking (cf seek above)

denied: rejected, declared untrue
denouement: final resolution of a story when the mystery is unveiled • **aloud:** in a loud voice (for everybody to hear)
• **midst:** middle • **breathless stillness:** total silence

beloved: my love, my darling • **the Fates:** the three goddesses who, according to Greek mythology, control human destinies
who would not hurt a fly! (same image in French): who is so gentle! • **poor chicken!** (fam): poor little darling!

– and when he hangs he will know and realize that it was Romaine who sent him to his death. And then – happiness, Beloved! Happiness at last!

There were experts present ready to swear that the handwriting was that of Romaine Heilger, but they were not needed. Confronted with the letter, Romaine broke down utterly and confessed everything. Leonard Vole had returned to the house at the time he said, twenty past nine. She had invented the whole story to ruin him.

With the collapse of Romaine Heilger, the case for the Crown collapsed also. Sir Charles called his few witnesses, the prisoner himself went into the box and told his story in a manly straightforward manner, unshaken by cross-examination.

The prosecution endeavoured to rally, but without great success. The judge's summing up was not wholly favourable to the prisoner, but a reaction had set in and the jury needed little time to consider their verdict.

'We find the prisoner not guilty.'

Leonard Vole was free!

Little Mr Mayherne hurried from his seat. He must congratulate his client.

He found himself polishing his pince-nez vigorously, and checked himself. His wife had told him only the night before that he was getting a habit of it. Curious things habits. People themselves never knew they had them.

An interesting case – a very interesting case. That woman, now, Romaine Heilger.

The case was dominated for him still by the exotic figure of Romaine Heilger. She had seemed a pale quiet woman in the house at Paddington, but in court she had flamed out against the sober background. She had flaunted herself like a tropical flower.

If he closed his eyes he could see her now, tall and vehement, her exquisite body bent forward a little, her right hand clenching and unclenching itself unconsciously all the time. Curious things, habits. That gesture of hers with the

happiness (noun); **happy** (adj)

handwriting: style of writing (form of the letters)

broke down: lost control of her emotions
utterly: totally, completely

ruin: destroy
collapse: breaking down (cf broke down above)
few: not numerous

manly: masculine ● **straightforward:** direct ● **unshaken:**
unperturbed
endeavoured: tried hard ● **rally:** regain credibility
summing up: review of the main points ● **wholly:** totally
set in: appeared

free (adj); **freedom** (noun), liberty
hurried: stood up in a rush ● **congratulate:** express
congratulations to; congratulate s.o. <u>on</u> sthg

checked himself: controlled himself
getting a habit of it: getting used to doing it

flamed out: made herself noticed by (potentially!) setting
the court on fire ● **against:** in contrast with ● **background:**
environment ● **flaunted herself:** opened up (for public
admiration)
exquisite: extremely beautiful

hand was her habit, he supposed. Yet he had seen someone else do it quite lately. Who was it now? Quite lately –

He drew in his breath with a gasp as it came back to him. *The woman in Shaw's Rents...*

He stood still, his head whirling. It was impossible – impossible – Yet, Romaine Heilger was an actress.

The KC came up behind him and clapped him on the shoulder.

'Congratulated our man yet? He's had a narrow shave, you know. Come along and see him.'

But the little lawyer shook off the other's hand.

He wanted one thing only – to see Romaine Heilger face to face.

He did not see her until some time later, and the place of their meeting is not relevant.

'So you guessed,' she said, when he had told her all that was in his mind. 'The face? Oh! That was easy enough, and the light of that gas jet was too bad for you to see the makeup.'

'But why – why –'

'Why did I play a lone hand?' She smiled a little, remembering the last time she had used the words.

'Such an elaborate comedy!'

'My friend – I had to save him. The evidence of a woman devoted to him would not have been enough – you hinted as much yourself. But I know something of the psychology of crowds. Let my evidence be wrung from me, as an admission, damning me in the eyes of the law, and a reaction in favour of the prisoner would immediately set in.'

'And the bundle of letters?'

'One alone, the vital one, might have seemed like a – what do you call it? – put-up job.'

'Then the man called Max?'

'Never existed, my friend.'

'I still think,' said little Mr Mayherne, in an aggrieved manner, 'that we could have got him off by the – er – normal procedure.'

'I dared not risk it. You see, you *thought* he was innocent –'

lately: not a long time ago, recently
drew in ... gasp: he was so shocked that he momentarily stopped breathing (probably remaining open-mouthed)
whirling: spinning round; *my head is in a whirl:* my mind is confused
clapped him: gave him a friendly hit
shoulder: joint between arm and body
he's had a narrow shave: *il l'a échappé belle!*
come along: come with me
shook off: refused to hold

is not relevant: needn't be mentioned
guessed: discovered, found out (the truth)
all that was in his mind: everything he thought

makeup: cosmetics used on the face to change its appearance

play a lone hand: act on my own, without any help

elaborate: complicated, intracte

you hinted as much: you mentioned it

crowds: big groups of people ● wring, wrung, **wrung:** obtained with difficulty

one alone: only one ● **what do you call it?:** used when trying to find the right words ● **a put-up job** (fam): sthg dishonestly arranged in advance

aggrieved: filled with resentment

I dared not: (here) I didn't want to ● **thought:** believed

'And you *knew* it? I see,' said little Mr Mayherne.

'My dear Mr Mayherne,' said Romaine, 'you do not see at all. I knew – he was guilty!'

know, **knew**, known: were aware of it ● **I see:** I understand

VOCABULARY

Voici environ 1 500 mots rencontrés dans les nouvelles, suivis du sens qu'ils ont dans celles-ci.

A

aback (be taken) être décontenancé
ability capacité
able to (be) être capable de
about to (be) être sur le point de
above all par-dessus tout
above board régulier, honnête
abroad à l'étranger
accomplished parfait
account compte rendu
accurate précis
acquaintance connaissance
act agir ; jouer au théâtre
actual exact, réel
actually en fait
add ajouter
admission aveu
adrift à l'abandon
advice conseils; **a piece of advice** un conseil
afraid (be) avoir peur ; **I am afraid** j'ai le regret de dire que…
afterwards après, plus tard
again de nouveau
against contre
aggrieved chagriné
ago (1 year) il y a (1 an)
agree être d'accord
airily avec désinvolture
alacrity empressement
alarm inquiétude
alike semblable
alive vivant
all over de partout ; terminé
allow autoriser, laisser
almost presque
alone seul
aloud à voix haute
already déjà
alter changer
altogether complètement
always toujours
amaze stupéfier, ébahir ; **amazing** stupéfiant
amount quantité ; **amount to** se résumer à
angry (with) en colère (contre)
answer répondre ; réponse
anyway de toute manière

appear sembler, paraître
applause applaudissements
apply for permission demander la permission
apron tablier
archbishop archevêque
ardent fervent, passionné
argue discuter
arise, arose, arisen surgir ; survenir
arm bras
arouse susciter
array assembler
as though comme si
as well autant ; aussi
ask demander
asleep endormi
assume supposer
assurance promesse
astonish étonner ; **astonishment** étonnement
at all du tout
at last enfin
at times parfois
attractive joli, attirant
aunt tante
Austrian autrichien
author auteur
avenging vengeur
averse to (be) répugner à
awarded (be) être récompensé, recevoir un prix
aware conscient
away (be) être absent
awful affreux

awkward délicat, difficile, embarrassant ;
awkwardly maladroitement

B

back dos
back out se retirer
background arrière-plan
backward ou **backwards** en arrière
bad, badly mal ; **from bad to worse** de pire en pire
bag sac
baize door porte capitonnée
balance équilibre
baldly abruptement
bang the door claquer la porte
bank holiday jour férié
bare nu
barrister avocat
barrow brouette **barrow-boy** marchand des quatre-saisons
base vil, indigne
beam-ends (to be on one's) être dans la dèche
bear (bore, borne) out confirmer, corroborer
bear down upon foncer sur
bear supporter ; **bear it**

(I can't) je ne peux pas le supporter

bearing rapport, relation

beast animal ; brute

beat (beat, beaten) about the bush tourner autour du pot

bed lit

beg supplier ; **I beg your pardon?** Comment?

begin, began, begun commencer

behave se comporter

behind derrière

belief croyance

believe croire

bell sonnette, sonnerie, cloche

belong to appartenir à

beloved (my) mon amour

bend, bent, bent se pencher ; **bend one's attention on** fixer son attention sur

beneath au-dessous de

beside à côté de ; **besides** de plus, en outre

best (the) le meilleur ; **do one's best** faire de son mieux

between entre

bewildered stupéfait

beyond au-delà de

bill affiche publicitaire

bit (a) un peu ; **not a bit** pas du tout

bit (cf **bite**)

bite, bit, bitten mordre

bitter amer ; **bitterness** amertume

blackguard canaille, fripouille

blackmail chantage

blank vide ; aveugle (mur)

bless bénir ; **blessed** béni

blind faux prétexte, couverture

blood sang ; **bloody** sanglant

bloodthirsty sanguinaire

blouse chemisier

blow coup

blow, blew, blown souffler ; **blow one's nose** se moucher

blur tache

bluster fanfaronner

board (on) à bord (bateau) ; en pension

boat bateau

body corps

bond lien

book registre

border frontière

borne (cf **bear**)

both tous les deux ; à la fois

bottom fond

bought (cf **buy**)

bound to (be) être quasi certain de

brain cerveau

break (broke, broken) down s'effondrer ; **break the news** annoncer la nouvelle

breakfast petit déjeuner
breast poitrine
breath respiration, souffle ; **breathless** oppressé
breathe respirer
bridge pont
brim bordure
bring, brought, brought apporter ; amener ; **bring up** élever
briskly brusquement
broke (cf **break**)
brood broyer du noir
brought (cf **bring**)
brow sourcil ; front ; sommet
building construction
bully malmener
bump secousse
bundle tas, liasse
burglar cambrioleur
burn, burnt, burnt or burned, burned brûler
burst éclat, accès
burst (burst, burst) into tears fondre en larmes ; **burst out with** laisser éclater ; **burst out laughing** éclater de rire
bury enterrer, enfouir
business affaire ; **a bad business** une sale affaire
busy occupé
butler majordome
buy, bought, bought acheter

bygone days (in) jadis
by-pass voie de contournement

C

call appeler, nommer ; **call upon s.o** rendre visite à qqn ; demander qqch à qqn
came (cf **come**)
cap bonnet, coiffe
capsize chavirer
care to daigner
careful (be) faire attention
carrion crow corneille noire ; charognard
carry porter
case affaire, procès
casually d'un air détaché
catch a glimpse of apercevoir
catch, caught, caught attraper, prendre
cautiously avec précaution
cease cesser
chaff taquiner
chance hasard
chap type
character personnage
charge with accuser de
charming charmant
charwoman femme de ménage
cheap bon marché
check oneself

s'interrompre
cheek joue ; culot
cheekbone pommette
cheerfully joyeusement
chemist pharmacien
chest poitrine, torse
chicken! (poor) pauvre poussin !, pauvre chéri !
child (pl **children**) enfant
chime in faire chorus
chit gamine
choose, chose, chosen choisir
chuckle gloussement
churlish grossier, impoli
claim demande
clap applaudir ; taper
clasp serrer
clean breast of it (make a) décharger sa conscience
clear disculper
clear-cut net, bien dessiné
clench serrer ; se serrer
clever intelligent ; **cleverness** intelligence
close (ad) près ; **closer** plus près ; **close quarters (at)** de très près
close (noun) fin
closely minutieusement
clue indice
coat manteau
coax amadouer
cod morue
coil boucle

cold froid ; **coldly** froidement ; **coldness** froideur
collapse s'effondrer ; effondrement
come, came, come venir ; **come away** s'en aller ; **come out** sortir ; **come off** réussir ; **come along!** venez !
comforter écharpe, étole
common ordinaire
composed calme, posé, maître de soi
conceal dissimuler
congratulate féliciter
consideration rémunération
constraint gêne
contemplate envisager
contrive s'arranger pour, s'efforcer de
convenient qui convient ; utile, pratique
convey an impression donner une impression
convicted inculpé
convinced convaincu
cook cuire ; cuisinier
core cœur (fig)
costs (at all) à tout prix
cough toux ; tousser
counsel juriste ; **counsel for the defence** avocat de la défense
count (take the) être mis K.O
country campagne

course (of) bien sûr
course of action ligne
  d'action
coward lâche
crayfish écrevisse,
  langouste
creased repassé
credence crédibilité
creep (cf **flesh**)
creep, crept, crept entrer
  furtivement
crooked de travers
croon chantonner
cross traverser
cross-examination
  double vérification ;
  contre-interrogatoire
crouch s'accroupir, se
  tapir
crowbar pied-de-biche
crowd foule ; masse
crunch crisser
cuff manchette (poignet
  de chemise)
cunningly
  malicieusement
cup day jour du Grand Prix
curb bord du trottoir
curse jurer ; maudire ;
  cursed maudit
curtain rideau
cut and dried fin prêt
cut, cut, cut couper ;
  cut in se faufiler ; **cut
  oneself adrift from so**
  se couper de qqn

D

daily quotidien
damage (sing) dégâts ;
  damaging préjudiciable
damn accabler ; **damning**
  accablant
dare oser ; **I dare say**
  sans aucun doute, je
  suppose, j'admets que
darling chéri
dash it all! bon sang !
  zut !
dastardly ignoble
dawn upon s.o venir à
  l'esprit de qqn
day off jour de congé
dazed hébété, abasourdi,
  sidéré
dead mort ; **stop dead**
  s'arrêter net
deadly mortellement
deaf sourd
deal (a great or a good)
  beaucoup
deal (dealt, dealt) with
  s'occuper de ; traiter de
deal table table de jeu
dealings (pl) transactions
dear cher ; **dear me!** mon
  Dieu !
dearest (the) le plus
  charmant
dearie chéri
death mort
deceased décédé
decreasing diminution
deed action

deeply profondément
delay retard ; **without delay** sans tarder
delighted ravi
delightfully délicieusement
deliver livrer
demur hésiter ; objecter
deny nier
derisive moqueur
deserve mériter
design (by) intentionnellement
devil diable ; **devilry** diablerie, maléfice
devoted dévoué
die mourir
dingy minable, miteux
dirty sale
disappear disparaître
disappointment déception
discover découvrir ; **discovery** découverte
discuss discuter
dishevelled ébouriffé
dislike antipathie
dismay consternation
dismiss balayer
disown désavouer
dispute discuter, contredire
distaste répugnance
disturb déranger ; **disturbed** perturbé
dock (in) au banc des accusés
dodderer vieux gâteux

doing (it's not my) je n'y suis pour rien
done with terminé
doomed perdu
doubled replié
doubtfully avec doute
downcast abattu
downstairs en bas
downwards (face) face contre terre
drag, drag out tirer, soutirer
dramatic théâtral ; spectaculaire
drank (cf **drink**)
draw aside écarter
draw blank échouer
draw, drew, drawn tirer ; **draw up** s'arrêter ; **draw a deep breath** respirer profondément
drawing dessin
drawing-room salon
drawn (cf **draw**)
dreadful épouvantable ; **dreadfully** terriblement
dress robe
dressed vêtu
drew (cf **draw**)
drift dériver ; se laisser influencer
drily sèchement
drink, drank, drunk boire
drive allée
drive, drove, driven conduire, mener ; **drive away** écarter ; **drive sthg home** faire

comprendre qqch à qqn
driver conducteur
drop laisser tomber ;
   goutte
drug drogue ; médicament
dry sec ; **dry as dust**
   ennuyeux comme la
   pluie
dubiously avec doute
duke duc
dumbfounded stupéfait,
   médusé
duty devoir
dying mourant

E

each chaque ; **each
   other** l'un l'autre,
   mutuellement
eagerness désir
   ardent ; **eagerly**
   passionnément,
   avidement
early tôt
earnest (in) pour de bon
earnestly sincèrement ;
   en toute bonne foi
earth terre ; **why on
   earth?** pourquoi
   diable ?
easy facile ; **easier** plus
   facile ; **easily** facilement
eat, ate, eaten manger
edible comestible
eerie inquiétant, sinistre
egg-shaped en forme

d'œuf
elderly âgé
elicit susciter
else autre
embarrassed gêné ;
   embarrassment gêne
emergency urgence
empty vide
enclosed inclus
end finir ; extrémité, fin
endeavour tenter de ;
   tentative
endless interminable
engaged fiancé ;
   engagement fiançailles
enlighten éclairer
enough assez
entangle empêtrer
epistle courrier
eve veille
even même ; **get even
   with s.o** prendre sa
   revanche sur qqn
evening soir
event événement ; **at all
   events** en tout cas
ever jamais
everyone tout le monde
everywhere partout
evidence témoignage ;
   **give evidence against
   s.o** témoigner contre
   qqn
evil-doing mauvais coup
evil-smelling nauséabond
evolve élaborer
expect s'attendre à ;
   supposer ; **expectantly**

dans l'expectative
expenditure dépense
explanation explication
eye œil ; observer
eyedrops gouttes pour les
 yeux
eyesight vue

F

face visage
fact fait
fail échouer, être
 déficient ; **failure** échec
faint faible ; léger ; **faintly**
 faiblement
fair blonde, jolie (fem) ;
 juste, honnête
fairly assez, relativement
faith foi, confiance ;
 faithful fidèle, dévoué
faithfully (yours)
 salutations distinguées
fall, fell, fallen tomber
fame célébrité
famous célèbre
fancy avoir l'impression
 que, imaginer ;
 imagination
fancy to s.o (take) se
 prendre d'affection pour
 qqn
far (so) jusqu'à présent
farmer fermier
fashion façon, manière
fast rapide, rapidement
fate destin

feature of (make a)
 mettre l'accent sur ;
 features traits
feel, felt, felt sentir,
 ressentir
feeling sentiment,
 sensation
feet (sing **foot) pieds**
fell (cf **fall**)
fellow camarade,
 compagnon, pair ; type
felt (cf **feel**)
fetch chercher
feverishly fébrilement
few (a) quelques
fidget gigoter
fierce violent
fight (fought, fought)
 hammer and tongs se
 battre à bras raccourcis
figure silhouette
fill remplir
find (found, found) out
 découvrir
finger doigt
fire feu
first premier ; en premier ;
 d'abord
fish out extirper
fish poisson ; **fishmonger**
 poissonnier
fist poing
fit in coïncider
flame out flamboyer
flash éclair
flat appartement
flaunt oneself s'épanouir
flesh chair ; **it made my**

flesh creep cela m'a donné la chair de poule
flick mouvement brusque
flickering vacillant
fling (flung, flung) back ouvrir brusquement ; **fling out** tendre
floor étage
florid haut en couleurs, ostentatoire
flow, flew, flown se déverser à flots
flung (cf **fling**)
flush rougir
fog brouillard ; **fogged** dans le brouillard, confus
foible travers, défaut
follow suivre ; **following** suivant
fond of (be) être prompt à ; aimer ; **fondness** attachement
fool idiot ; **foolish** insensé
foot (pl **feet**) pied
footsteps bruits de pas
foppishly de manière sophistiquée ; comme un dandy
forbid, forbade, forbidden interdire
foreign étranger
forget, forgot, forgotten oublier
forgive, forgave, forgiven pardonner
formidable impressionnant, redoutable
forth en avant
fortunately heureusement
forward en avant
fought (cf **fight**)
found (cf **find**)
frankness franchise
free libérer ; libre
frightened (be) avoir peur
frightful effrayant ; **frightfully** terriblement
frisk fouiller
frown froncer les sourcils
fungus, pl **fungi** champignon
fur coat manteau de fourrure
furnished meublé
further plus précis
fuss (make a) faire des histoires

G

gagged bâillonné
game jeu
gasp suffocation
gate barrière
gather deviner, déduire, conclure ; **I gather** Je suppose
gaunt émacié, décharné
gentle doux ; **the gentlest** le plus doux
genuine vrai, authentique ; **genuinely**

sincèrement

get (got, got) away s'enfuir ; **get even with** prendre sa revanche sur qqn

get hold of se saisir de ; **get at sth** comprendre qqch

get in monter (véhicule) ; **get on** s'entendre ; **get s.o off** tirer qqn d'affaire

gingerly avec précaution

give way abandonner

give, gave, given donner ; **give in** abandonner ; **give rise to** engendrer

glad heureux, content

glance regard ; **glance at** jeter un coup d'œil à

glass verre

glimpse coup d'œil

gloves gants

go, went, gone aller ; **go by** se fier à ; **go off** partir, se déclencher ; **go on** poursuivre ; **go over** récapituler ; **go after** courir après ; **go for** tomber sur

God! My God! mon Dieu ! **Thank God!** Dieu merci ! **God forbid that** Dieu me garde bien de

gold or, doré ; **golden** en or

good-looking beau

gory sanglant

gossip commérer ; commérage

granted (take it for) considérer comme allant de soi

granted that étant entendu que

grasp saisir

grateful reconnaissant

grave tombe

gravel gravillon

greasepaint fard gras (maquillage de scène)

greatest (the) le (la) plus grand(e)

grew (cf **grow**)

grief chagrin

grim sévère, sinistre

grin large sourire

groan grogner

ground terrain, domaine

grow, grew, grown croître, grandir ; **grow stronger** s'amplifier

grudgingly à contrecœur

guess deviner

guilt culpabilité ; **guilty** coupable

gurgle gargouiller

gutter caniveau

H

haddock aiglefin

hail a taxi héler un taxi

hair (sing) cheveux

half à moitié ; demi

half-breathe prononcer à demi-mot

halting hésitant

hammer and tongs à bras raccourcis, avec violence

hand (on the other) d'autre part

handle manipuler, manœuvrer, prendre en main

hands up! haut les mains !

handsome élégant

hand-writing écriture, graphie

hang, hung, hung or **hanged, hanged** pendre

hangings tentures

happen arriver (événement)

happiness bonheur ; **happily** heureusement

hard dur

hard up (fam) dans la dèche

hardly à peine, difficilement ; **hardly ever** très rarement

hasten se hâter

hastily précipitamment

hate détester

hatred haine

haunts (plur) repaire

have it in for s.o avoir une dent contre qqn

head tête ; **headache** mal de tête

heap tas

hear, heard, heard entendre

heart cœur ; **hearty** chaleureux ; **heart-rending** qui fend le cœur

heaven's sake (for) pour l'amour du ciel ; **heaven knows** Dieu seul sait

heavy violent ; lourd

hedge haie

heed of (take no) ne pas faire attention à

held (cf **hold**)

help aider ; **I can't help it!** je ne peux pas m'en empêcher !

helplessly désespérément

hence d'où

hide, hid, hidden cacher

high haut, élevé ; **highly** hautement

high horse (to be on one's) monter sur ses grands chevaux

High Street rue principale

high-pitched haut perché

hill colline

hinge on dépendre de

hint faire allusion à, insinuer, suggérer ; indice

hit (hit, hit) upon trouver

hoarse rauque

hoax canular

hold of (get) mettre la main sur

hold, held, held tenir ; **hold out** tendre ; présenter ; **get hold of** trouver, dénicher

home maison, foyer

hood capot (voiture)

hope espérer ; espoir ; **hopeless** désespéré ; **hopelessly** désespérément

hotly violemment

household word (a) un nom que tout le monde connaît

however cependant

huge énorme

humble pie (eat) faire des excuses humiliantes

hundred cent

hunt about for sthg être à la recherche de qqch

hurry se précipiter ; **hurriedly** avec empressement

hurt a fly (he would not) il ne ferait pas de mal à une mouche

husband mari, époux

hussy garce

I

icy glacé

idiosyncrasy particularité

idle oisif

ill malade ; **be taken ill** tomber malade

impotent impuissant

impress sthg on s.o faire bien comprendre qqch à qqn

inch pouce = 2,54 cm

income revenu

increasingly de plus en plus

indeed en effet, certes

infatuated with entiché de

ingenious ingénieux, astucieux

inquire demander

insanity folie

inside à l'intérieur (de)

instance (for) par exemple

instead of à la place de, au lieu de

institution hôpital psychiatrique

intent on (be) être résolu à

intricate compliqué, complexe

introduce présenter

island île

J

jet (gas) brûleur de gazinière

jewel bijou

join in participer à

joke plaisanterie
jolly (fam) sacré
jump sauter

K

KC = King's Counsel
avocat de la Couronne
keen vif, aiguisé
keep (kept, kept) garder ;
keep + ing ne pas
cesser de ; **keep to**
s'en tenir à
keep sthg back garder le
silence sur qqch ; **keep
straight** rester dans le
droit chemin
kerb bord du trottoir
kick coup de pied, ruade ;
kick out jeter, éjecter
kid gosse, gamin
kill tuer
kind genre, sorte
kindly bienveillant
kindness bonté
kiss embrasser
knee genou
kneel, knelt, knelt se
mettre à genoux
knew (cf **know**)
knife couteau ; **get one's
knife into s.o** en avoir
après qqn
knit tricoter ; **knitting**
tricot
knock on the door
frapper à la porte

knockout K.O
know, knew, known
connaître, savoir
knowledge connaissance

L

lack manque ; manquer
de
lad garçon, gars
lamb agneau ; personne
innocente
lap genoux; giron
last dernier ; **at last** enfin
latched fermé à clef
late of autrefois domicilié
à
lately récemment
later plus tard
latter (the) le dernier
nommé
laugh rire ; **laugh at s.o**
rire de qqn
law loi ; **lawyer** homme de
loi, avocat
lay (cf **lie**)
lead, led, led mener
**lean, leant, leant (or
leaned, leaned)** se
pencher
leap sursaut, bond
leap, lept, lept or **leaped,
leaped** sauter
**learn, learnt, learnt (or
learned, learned)**
apprendre
least (at) au moins ; **the**

least le moindre

leave it to me! laisse-moi faire

leave sthg alone laisser tomber qqch

leave, left, left laisser ; quitter, partir

led (cf **lead**)

leer regard méchant ; **leer at** lorgner sur

left (cf **leave**)

left gauche

leg jambe ; **he hasn't got a leg to stand on** il ne peut s'appuyer sur rien

lend, lent, lent prêter

leper lépreux

less moins

let s.o out mettre qqn hors de cause

let, let, let laisser, permettre

lethal mortel

level régulier

license permis, autorisation

lie mentir ; mensonge ; **pack of lies, tissue of lies** tissu de mensonges

lie, lay, lain être posé ; être allongé ; se trouver

life vie

lift lever

light lumière ; **ray of light** rayon de lumière

lighted or **lit** éclairé

like comme

likely probable ; **likely to (be)** être susceptible de

lip lèvre

live vivre, habiter, demeurer

living (make one's) gagner sa vie

load charger

lock fermer à clef

lone hand (play a) mener une action solitaire

lonely solitaire

longer plus longtemps

look after s'occuper de ; **look like** ressembler à

loose desserré, détaché

Lord Dieu ; **by the Lord!** Mon Dieu !

loud fort ; **louder** plus fort ; **loudly** fort

lovely charmant

low bas **low water** marée basse ; point le plus bas (fig)

lower inférieur ; **the lowest** le plus bas

luck chance ; **rough luck** malchance

lucky chanceux ; **it's a lucky thing** c'est une bonne chose

lunge out asséner (un coup)

lying (cf **lie**)

M

M.P = Member of Parliament député

mad fou ; **madhouse** asile d'aliénés

maid or **maidservant** servante

mainly principalement

make (made, made) away with oneself se donner la mort

make up to s.o faire des avances à qqn

makeup maquillage

malicious malveillant, méchant

manage to réussir à

manly viril

manner façon, manière

mark marque, empreinte

master maître ; maîtriser

matter question, sujet ; **matter of fact (as a)** en fait

matter (it doesn't) ça n'a pas d'importance

matter (what's the) qu'est-ce qui se passe ?

mattress matelas

mean, meant, meant vouloir dire, signifier

means (pl) moyen (noun)

meaning signification

medicine médicament

meekly humblement

meet, met, met rencontrer

memory mémoire, souvenir

mere simple ; **merely** simplement

mesh maille

met (cf **meet**)

middle-aged d'âge mûr

midst of (in the) au milieu de

mighty + adj sacrément, rudement

mild doux, calme

milkman laitier

mind esprit ; **make up one's mind** se décider ; **change one's mind** changer d'avis

mislead, misled, misled induire en erreur

miss manquer, rater

missing disparu

mistake erreur ; **mistake, mistook, mistaken** mal interpréter

misunderstand, misunderstood, misunderstood mal comprendre

mixed up with (be) être mêlé à

moan grommeler

money argent ; **moneymaker** homme d'affaires

month mois

moody maussade

more or less plus ou moins

moreover de plus

mostly principalement

motto ligne de conduite, devise

mud boue

muffled assourdi, étouffé (son)

mulish têtu

murder meurtre, homicide

mushroom champignon

mutter marmonner, murmurer

mystified perplexe

N

name (Christian) prénom

narrative récit

narrow se rétrécir ; **narrowly** de près

nasty mauvais, méchant

near près de ; **nearly** presque

neat propre et net

neck cou

need besoin ; avoir besoin de ; **needed** nécessaire

neither non plus ; **neither...nor** ni...ni

nephew neveu

nerve to do sth (have the) avoir le culot de faire qqch

nerves nerfs ; **a mass of nerves** une boule de nerfs

nestle se nicher

net filet

never mind cela ne fait rien

nevertheless néanmoins

new neuf, nouveau

next suivant ; puis, ensuite

nice gentil, agréable

nickname surnom

no sooner...than à peine ...que

nobody personne

nod acquiescer

nonsense (sing) bêtises, idioties

nose nez

note billet

nothing rien

notice remarquer

novel roman

now and then (every) de temps en temps

nowadays à l'heure actuelle, de nos jours

number is up (my) je suis fichu, mon compte est bon

nurse infirmière

O

oath juron

obtain obtenir

obvious évident ; **obviously** de toute évidence

occur arriver, se produire ; venir à l'esprit

odd étrange, bizarre ; **the odds** la probabilité
offender coupable
offer proposer
once and for all une fois pour toutes
once une fois ; autrefois ; **once more** une fois de plus ; **at once** immédiatement
only seul
open ouvrir
opportunity occasion, chance
order permis ; prescrire
otherwise autrement
ought to (he) il devrait
outer extérieur
outlandish exotique
outlive s.o survivre à qqn
out-of-the-way reculé, retiré
outside à l'extérieur
outsider personne extérieure
outsize gigantesque
over au-dessus de ; **over and over** encore et encore
overcome, overcame, overcome surmonter
overwhelm accabler, submerger
overwrought à bout de nerfs
owe devoir (argent)
own propre, personnel ; posséder

P

pace up and down faire les cent pas
pad bloc-notes
paid (cf **pay**)
paint peindre
pamper choyer
paper journal
parcel paquet
parlourmaid femme de chambre
party soirée, fête
pattern modèle, patron (couture)
pay (paid, paid) s.o a visit rendre visite à qqn
pay s.o the compliment to faire l'honneur à qqn de
peaceful calme, paisible
pedestrian piéton
peep jeter un coup d'œil
peer scruter
pencil crayon
perch perche (poisson)
perform accomplir
performance représentation
perhaps peut-être
perjury faux témoignage
perspiration transpiration
pick up ramasser
picture image, film ; **pictures** cinéma
piece morceau
pike brochet
pillow on reposer sur

pin épingle ; **you could have heard a pin drop** on aurait entendu une mouche voler

pinned épinglé

pit fauteuils d'orchestre (théâtre)

pitiful pitoyable

pity (it's a) c'est dommage

place lieu, endroit ; **take place** avoir lieu

plain simple, clair, évident ; sincère

plan projet

plate assiette

play a part jouer un rôle

plead plaider

pleased content, satisfait

plot intrigue

pocket poche, vide-poche (voiture)

pocketbook portefeuille

point out montrer du doigt ; faire remarquer

polish frotter, nettoyer

ponderous pesant et solennel

poor pauvre ; **poorly** chichement

post-mortem autopsie

postpone différer

pot of money (make a pretty little) gagner une fortune

pound livre sterling

pour verser ; **pour out** vider

power puissance

prayer prière

preposterous absurde, ridicule

press appuyer

presume se permettre de

pretty joli ; **pretty + adj** plutôt, assez

previous précédent ; **previously** précédemment

price prix, coût ; **(not) at any price** à aucun prix

pride fierté ; **pride oneself on** se féliciter de

print imprimer

prize-fighter boxeur professionnel

proceed avancer, circuler

proceedings débats

profane irrespectueux

proper convenable

property propriété

proposal proposition en mariage

prosecution accusation

protrude dépasser, faire saillie

proud fier

ptomaine poisoning intoxication alimentaire

pull tirer sur

pulse pouls

purl maille à l'envers (tricot)

purple violet, pourpre

pursue suivre ; poursuivre

put it over on s.o faire marcher qqn

put up the banns publier les bans

put, put, put mettre ; **put away** mettre de côté

put-up job coup monté

puzzled perplexe

Q

quarrel dispute

quaver parler d'une voix chevrotante

queen reine

queer bizarre, étrange

quell réprimer

quick rapide ; **quickness** rapidité ; **quickly** rapidement

quick-wittedness vivacité d'esprit

quid (fam) livre sterling

quiet silencieux ; **quietly** silencieusement ; **quieten** réduire au silence

quite tout à fait

quizzical narquois

quote citer

R

raise lever

rally reprendre le dessus

ramble errer, déambuler ;

rambling talk paroles insensées

ramshackle délabré

ran (cf **run**)

rang (cf **ring**)

rank avoir le rang de, se classer

rate (at any) en tout cas

rather plutôt, assez

rave at s.o s'emporter contre qqn

reach atteindre

read, read, read lire

realize se rendre compte de

recall rappeler, se rappeler

recipe recette

recoil reculer, hésiter

recover ramasser ; retrouver

refined raffiné

reflect réfléchir

regard considérer

relative membre de la famille

relent se radoucir

relevant significatif

relief soulagement

relieve soulager

reluctance réticence ; **reluctantly** à contre-cœur

remain rester, demeurer

remember se rappeler, se souvenir de

remind s.o of sthg
rappeler qqch à qqn

remote éloigné

reply répondre

report rapport, compte
rendu

request demande

resource (as a last) en
dernier recours

retie renouer

retort répliquer

rickety branlant, bancal

rid oneself of se
débarrasser de

ride (rode, ridden) a bus
se déplacer en bus

right bien, correct, exact

ring, rang, rung sonner ;
ring up téléphoner

rise, rose, risen se lever

rode (cf **ride**)

rope corde

rose (cf **rise**)

row rang, rangée

rubbish (sing): bêtises

ruffian voyou, brute

ruined anéanti

rule (as a) en règle
générale

run période

run, ran, run away
s'échapper

rung (cf **ring**)

rush se précipiter

rustle bruissement

S

sack (fam) virer

safe sain et sauf ; **safely**
sans risque, à coup sûr

sag s'affaisser

said (cf **say**)

sail naviguer

sake (for my) par égard
pour moi

same (the) le même,
semblable

sank (cf **sink**)

save sauver

saw (cf **see**)

say, said, said dire ; **say
so** confirmer

scan parcourir du regard

scapegrace vaurien

scarf écharpe

scarlet écarlate

Scotland Écosse

scrawl griffonner

scream hurler ; hurlement

seat siège

securities valeurs, titres
financiers

see, saw, seen voir

seek, sought, sought
chercher

seem sembler, paraître

seldom rarement

selfish égoïste

sell, sold, sold vendre

send, sent, sent envoyer ;
send for s.o envoyer
chercher qqn

sensible sensé, raisonnable

sensitive sensible

sent (cf **send**)

sentenced to condamné à

set (set, set) dead against être nettement défavorable à

set, set, set figer ; **set in** surgir

settle down s'installer

settle s.o régler son compte à qqn

several plusieurs

shabby miteux

shade pointe, soupçon

shake, shook, shaken secouer, remuer, ébranler ; **shake off** se libérer de ; **shake hands** serrer la main

shaky tremblant

shape forme, apparence ; prendre forme

sharply durement ; **sharpness** dureté

shave (he's had a narrow) il l'a échappé belle !

sheet of paper feuille de papier

shifty fuyant

shook (cf **shake**)

shoot, shot, shot tirer un coup de revolver

shoot out the hand pointer du doigt

short court ; **shortly** bientôt

shorthand sténographie

short-sighted myope

short story nouvelle

shot (cf **shoot**)

shoulder épauler ; épaule

shout at s.o crier sur qqn

show, showed, showed or **shown** montrer

shrewd perspicace

shuffle traîner des pieds

shut, shut, shut fermer ; **shut s.o up or away** enfermer qqn ; **shut oneself up** se renfermer sur soi-même

side côté

sidle marcher furtivement

sigh soupirer ; soupir

sight vue, vision ; **by sight** de vue

silly stupide ; **silliness** stupidité

simmer mijoter

single célibataire ; seul et unique

sink, sank, sunk chavirer ; **sink down** s'affaisser

sitting-room salon

skin peau

slack ralentir le pas

slatternly négligé

sleeve manche

slender mince

slight léger ; **slightly** légèrement ; **the slightest** le moindre

slip glisser

slower plus lent

slum taudis

smash (go) être brisé, voler en éclats

smile sourire

smoke fumée

smother étouffer

smoulder couver (émotion)

snarl dire d'un ton hargneux

sneer ricaner ; **sneeringly** en ricanant

so long as tant que

society girl fille de la haute société

softly doucement

solicitor avocat

solve résoudre

some time un certain temps

something quelque chose

somewhat quelque peu

son fils

soothe apaiser

sought (cf **seek**)

soul âme

spare épargner

speak, spoke, spoken parler

spectacles lunettes

speech parole

speed vitesse

spell, spelt, spelt signifier

spicy corsé

spied (cf **spy**)

spike s.one's guns mettre des bâtons dans les roues à qqn

spite of (in) malgré

spoil, spoilt, spoilt gâcher

spoke (cf **speak**)

spoonful cuillerée

spot lieu, endroit ; tache

spring (sprang, sprung) back faire un bond en arrière

spring (sprang, sprung) up se lever précipitamment

spy upon s.o épier qqn

squalid sordide

squeal cri aigu

stage scène ; **stage property** accessoire de théâtre

stain tache ; **stained with** taché de

staircase cage d'escalier

stairs escaliers

stamp timbre

stand (stood, stood) up against se mesurer à, se battre contre

stand it (I can't) je ne peux pas le supporter

stand, stood, stood se tenir debout ; **stand up** se lever

stare at fixer

start commencer ;
sursauter ; **start off** se
mettre en route

startling ahurissant ;
startled ahuri, stupéfait

starve mourir de faim

state état

statement déclaration

stay rester ; séjourner

steady régulier ; **steadily**
régulièrement ;
fermement

steal (stole, stolen) over
s'insinuer

stealthy furtif

step pas ; marche ; **step
in** monter (voiture) ;
retrace one's steps
revenir sur ses pas

sternly sévèrement

stick, stuck, stuck coller ;
stick up for prendre la
défense de

stick together se serrer
les coudes

still immobile ; toujours,
encore ; **stillness**
calme, silence

stitch maille de tricot

stone pierre

stood (cf **stand**)

stoop se baisser

stop dead s'arrêter net

story histoire

stove poêle

straight tout droit,
directement ;
straightforward direct

strangle étrangler

stray errant ; isolé, rare

stream flot

strength force

stride, strode, stridden
marcher à grands pas

strike, struck, struck
frapper

string ficelle ; **string bag**
filet à provisions

strive to, strove, striven
s'efforcer de

strode (cf **stride**)

strong fort ; **strongest
(the)** le plus fort

strong-willed déterminé,
volontaire

struggle (sing) difficultés

stuck (cf **stick**)

student étudiant

study bureau (pièce) ;
étudier

stuff truc, machin

succeed in + ing réussir
à

suffer souffrir

sullenly d'un air
maussade

summing up résumé (des
faits)

summons appel

sunset coucher de soleil

supper souper

support corroborer

surge déferler

swallow avaler

swear, swore, sworn jurer

sweat sueur ; **the sweat broke out** la sueur perla
sweep virage
swerve dévier
swill sthg down boire à grandes gorgées
swindle escroquer

T

tablespoon cuillère à soupe
taint défaut, tare
take, took, taken prendre ; **take away** éloigner ; **take down** prendre en note
talk parler ; bavardage
tall grand
tankard chope, pot à bière
tansy tea décoction de tanaisie
tassel pompon
tattered en lambeaux
tear larme ; **tearfully** en larmes
tear, tore, torn déchirer
teeth (sing **tooth)** dents
tell, told, told dire, raconter
telling instructif, parlant
temper tempérament
tenant occupant, locataire
testimony témoignage
thank remercier
thick voice voix étouffée

think, thought, thought penser ; **think sthg over** réfléchir à qqch
third troisième
thoroughly de fond en comble
though bien que, quoique
thought pensée ; **thoughtfully** pensivement
thousand mille
threat menace ; **threaten** menacer
threshold seuil
threw (cf **throw**)
throat gorge ; **clear one's throat** s'éclaircir la gorge
throb vibrer
throw, threw, thrown jeter, lancer ; **throw over** abandonner
thumb pouce
tide marée
tie lier, nouer ; **tie up** ligoter
tightly très tendu, serré
tiny minuscule
tired fatigué ; **be tired of** en avoir assez de
title titre
together ensemble ; **get on together** s'entendre (bien ou mal)
toiler personne qui travaille dur
told (cf **tell**)
tomorrow demain

toneless atone
tongue langue
tonight ce soir
took (cf **take**)
top haut
tore (cf **tear**)
toss lancer
touchy susceptible
touring car voiture de tourisme
tourniquet garrot
towards vers, en direction de
track chemin, voie, piste
trail round traîner
trap piège
treat négocier
trial procès ; **to commit s.o for trial** mettre qqn en accusation
trick farce, blague ; ruse, stratagème ; tic
trifle babiole ; **trifle (a)** légèrement, un peu
trifling insignifiant
trigger gâchette
trouble problème **be in trouble** avoir des ennuis
trousers (pl) pantalon
truck with (have no) refuser d'avoir affaire à
true vrai ; exact
trump up forger, inventer
trust faire confiance à
truth vérité ; **speak the truth** dire la vérité
truthful sincère ;

truthfully avec sincérité
try essayer ; **try one's best** faire de son mieux
tube station station de métro
twice deux fois
twitch (nervous) tic nerveux
type typographie, écriture
type-writer machine à écrire

U

unable incapable
unbearable insupportable
unbia(s)sed impartial
uncle oncle
unclench desserrer, se desserrer
unconnected with sans lien avec
understand, understood, understood comprendre
understudy doubler un acteur
uneasy mal à l'aise ; **uneasiness** malaise, gêne
unemotional impassible
uneventful où jamais rien ne se passe
unexpected inattendu
unfathomable insondable, insoutenable
unforeseen imprévu

unfortunately
malheureusement
unhappy malheureux
unimportant sans
importance, insignifiant
unkind peu gentil ; peu
aimable
unless à moins que
unlike dissemblable,
différent
unlikely improbable
unluckily
malheureusement
unmade défait
unpleasant désagréable
unsavoury répugnant,
louche
unshaken stoïque ;
unshakable
inébranlable
unsympathetic peu
amical, hostile
untidy désordonné
untie dénouer
until jusqu'à ; **not until**
pas avant
unusual inhabituel
up and down de haut en
bas
upset perturbé, contrarié
upstairs en haut, à l'étage
upstanding bien bâti,
costaud
urge s.o to do sth
pousser qqn à faire
qqch
use utilisation, usage ;
utiliser

use (it's no) + ing cela ne
sert à rien de
useful utile
usher faire entrer
usual habituel
utmost extrême
utter émettre
utterly totalement

V

vagary caprice
vegetable végétal
velvet velours
view of (in) à cause de
view point de vue,
appréciation, vision
vindicate justifier,
défendre
voice voix

W

wag remuer, agiter
wages (pl) salaire
waif enfant abandonné
wait (for) attendre
wake, woke (or waked),
woken up réveiller
walk marcher
want vouloir
warmly chaleureusement
warn avertir
waste time perdre du
temps
watch observer ; montre

watchdog gardien, gardienne

wave signe de la main

waver hésiter, balancer

way chemin, passage ; façon, manière ; **give way** abandonner

way out issue, porte de sortie

weak faible ; **weaken** faiblir

wealthy riche

weapon arme

wear, wore, worn porter sur soi (vêtement)

weariness lassitude

weather temps (qu'il fait)

week semaine

well behaved qui se comporte bien

well off riche

went (cf **go**)

wet pluvieux

wheel volant ; **wheel round** se retourner brusquement

wheezy poussif, sifflant

wherever où que ce soit

whether si

whilst pendant que

whine gémir

whirl tourner

whisper chuchoter

whistle siffler

Whitsuntide Pentecôte

whole entier ; **wholly** entièrement, tout à fait

wicked méchant ; **wickedness** méchanceté

wide large, largement

wide-open spaces grands espaces naturels

widespread important, étendu

wife épouse

wild effréné ; **wildly** furieusement

wilful murder meurtre avec préméditation

win, won won gagner

will testament

willing volontaire

wind, wound, wound

or **winded, winded**
enrouler
winding sinueux
window fenêtre ; vitrine
wipe essuyer
wire envoyer un télégramme
wise avisé
wish souhaiter
wistfulness nostalgie,
regret
withal de plus
within en l'espace de
without sans
**witness for the
prosecution** témoin à
charge
wits' end (be at one's) ne
plus savoir que faire
wit(s) esprit, intelligences
astuce
woke up (cf **wake**)
won (cf **win**)
wonder se demander
wonderful merveilleux
word parole, mot ; **my
word!** ma parole !
wore (cf **wear**)

work fonctionner
world monde
worry s'inquiéter ;
worried inquiet
worse pire
worst (the) le pire
worth (be) valoir
wound (cf **wind**)
wrapped absorbé
wrath colère
wretched malheureux
wring, wrung, wrung
extorquer
wrist poignet
write, wrote, written
écrire
wrung (cf **wring**)

Y

year année
yet cependant ; **not yet**
pas encore
young jeune

LIRE EN ANGLAIS

TEXTE ORIGINAL ANNOTÉ

A Fruitful Sunday
and other short stories

Agatha Christie

Le Livre de Poche

LIRE EN ANGLAIS

TEXTE ORIGINAL ANNOTÉ

Thirteen Modern English and American Short Stories

R. Bradbury / T. Capote /
R. Dahl / G. Greene /
J. Updike…

Le Livre de Poche

LIRE EN ANGLAIS

TEXTE ORIGINAL ANNOTÉ

English
Crime Stories
of Today

Ruth Rendell, Agatha Christie,
Frederick Forsyth,
Antonia Fraser

Le Livre
de Poche

PAPIER À BASE DE
FIBRES CERTIFIÉES

Le Livre de Poche s'engage pour
l'environnement en réduisant
l'empreinte carbone de ses livres.
Celle de cet exemplaire est de :
250 g éq. CO_2
Rendez-vous sur
www.livredepoche-durable.fr

Achevé d'imprimer en mars 2013 en Espagne par
Black Print CPI Iberica, S.L.
Sant Andreu de la Barca (08740)
Dépôt légal 1ère publication : octobre 2006
Édition 06: mars 2013
LIBRAIRIE GÉNÉRALE FRANÇAISE – 31, rue de Fleurus – 75278 Paris Cedex 06